Market Rebels

To

Diego

Be a rebel

Hyy

HAYAGREEVA RAO

MARKET REBELS

How Activists Make or Break Radical Innovations

PRINCETON UNIVERSITY PRESS   Princeton and Oxford

Published by Princeton University Press, 41 William Street, Princeton,
New Jersey 08540

In the United Kingdom: Princeton University Press, 6 Oxford Street,
Woodstock, Oxfordshire OX20 1TW

Library of Congress Cataloging-in-Publication Data
Rao, Hayagreeva, 1959–
    Market rebels : how activists make or break radical innovations /
    Hayagreeva Rao.
        p.   cm.
    Includes bibliographical references and index.
    ISBN 978-0-691-13456-7 (hardcover : alk. paper)   1. Social movements.
    2. Social action.   3. Social change.   4. Capitalism—Social aspects.
    I. Title.
    HM881.R36   2009
    303.48'—dc22   2008022094

British Library Cataloging-in-Publication Data is available

This book has been composed in Minion and Scala Sans

Printed on acid-free paper. ∞

press.princeton.edu

Printed in the United States of America

10 9 8 7 6 5 4 3 2 1

For Sadhna

Contents

Preface

The origins of this book are both profoundly personal and social. I became a teenager in India at a time of mobilization and contention in the mid-1970s. I lived in Visakhapatnam—a city where collective mobilization in the form of strikes and train blockades persuaded central planners in New Delhi to build a steel plant there. Later, the imposition of a state of emergency by Prime Minister Indira Gandhi also evoked social protest, which was suppressed but still found expression in elections where she was routed. Subsequently, collective action played a significant role in my experience as a student of industrial relations and human-resource management at a business school in India (XLRI, Jamshedpur) when the cafeteria workers went on strike and my classmates who were leading the student association mobilized us to cook food and clean dishes in a (successful) bid to break the strike by cafeteria workers.

My doctoral education in organizational behavior at Case Western Reserve University also emphasized the mobilization of employees to further organizational change. One day, however, a chance visit to the wrong floor of Sears Library led me to discover *The Horseless Age* and to discern how the automobile, once vilified by farmers and anti-speed opponents, became accepted when auto enthusiasts organized themselves into clubs and scheduled reliability contests to demonstrate the value of the car. At the same time my dissertation on savings and loans led to conversations with Mohan Reddy, one of my committee members and, above all, a generous friend who whetted my appetite for the study of "non-market" approaches in the fields of marketing and economics. My intellectual collaboration with Heather Haveman and Jerry Davis was formative in thinking about cultural change and identity processes.

My interest in social movements was systematized when I took a much-needed sabbatical from Emory University to the business school at the University of Michigan at the invitation of Jane Dutton, who has since successfully launched a social movement of her own on positive organizing. The wonderful intellectual climate at Michigan with its interdisciplinary ethos provided an opportunity for me to engage with the literature on social movements. Mayer Zald, a deeply knowledgeable and generous sociologist, was friend, mentor, and foil, and our many stimulating conversations expanded my intellectual horizons. Calvin Morrill, a sociologist at the University of California–Irvine, joined us, and our collaboration was not only successful but provided the foundations for my work on movements and markets even after I moved to the Kellogg School.

Since then, other collaborations have provided the basis for research on how movements shaped markets in a wide variety of contexts. My work with Philippe Monin and Rodolphe Durand allowed me to study how movements re-shaped French cuisine. Working with Paul Ingram enabled me to understand the anti–chain store movement and the links between mobilization and diffusion. Research with Henrich Greve and Jo-Ellen Pozner allowed me to understand the low-power FM radio movement, and collaborations with Klaus Weber and L. G. Thomas provided a window into the anti-biotechnology movement in Germany. Finally, a project with Joe Porac, Jim Wade, Tim Pollock, and Yuri Mishina enabled me to appreciate the investor rights movement along with my own work on investor relations departments.

Some of the chapters in this book rely on my previously published work. They have been rewritten for the general reader rather than the specialist in organizational sociology. Chapter 2 draws on "The Social Construction of Reputation: Certification Contests, Legitimation and the Survival of the Organizations in the American Automobile Industry, 1985–1912," *Strategic Management Journal* 15 (1994): 29–44, and "The Power of Public Competition: Promoting Cognitive and Sociopolitical Legitimacy through Certification Contests," in *The Entrepreneurship Dynamic*, ed. Kaye Schoonhoven and Elaine Romanelli (Stanford: Stanford University Press, 2001), 262–85. Chapter 4 draws on my essays coauthored with Philippe Monin and Rodolphe Durand, "Institutional Change in Tocqueville: Nouvelle Cuisine as an Identity Movement in French Gastronomy," *American Journal of Sociology* 108:4 (2003): 795–843, and "Border Crossing: Bricolage and the Erosion of Categorical Boundaries in French Gastronomy," *American Sociological Review* 70:6 (2005): 968–91. Chapter 5 draws partially on my essay coauthored with K. Sivakumar, "Institutional Sources of Boundary Spanning Structures: The Establishment of Investor Relations Departments in the Fortune 500," *Organization Science* 10 (1999): 27–42, and a joint study with Yuri Mishina, Tim Pollock, Jim Wade, and Joe Porac, "The Use of Anti-Management Resolutions by Corporate Gadflies: Choosing Targets for Delegitimation by Peripheral Actors" (working paper, Michigan State University, 2007). Chapter 6 leans on my essay with Paul Ingram, "Store Wars: The Enactment and Repeal of Anti–Chain Store Laws," *American Journal of Sociology* 110 (2004): 446–87. Chapter 7 relies on a study with Klaus Weber and L. G. Thomas, "From Streets to Suites: The Impact of the German Anti-Biotech Movement on German Pharmaceutical Firms" (working paper, Kellogg School of Management, 2007).

I received encouragement from colleagues Glenn Carroll, Mike Hannan, and Jeff Pfeffer at the Graduate School of Business at Stanford to consolidate my research into a book aimed at the general reader. Glenn Carroll generously shared material on microbrewing, and Mike Hannan helped sharpen my thinking at key stages. Other Stanford colleagues who provided moral support and practical advice include Robert Burgelman, Chip Heath, Doug McAdam, John Meyer, Chiqui Ramirez, Susan Olzak, Woody Powell, Dick Scott, Steve Barley, and Robert Sutton. The book took concrete shape after helpful conversations with these generous and insightful people. An ongoing project with Giacomo Negro, Mike Hannan, and Ming Leung on contention and innovation in the Barolo wine district in Italy also provided fillip to the book (as well as wonderful trips to the north of Italy). Chip Heath, Paul Ingram, Calvin Morrill, Sarah Soule,

Robert Sutton, and Mayer Zald generously read drafts of the manuscript and proffered helpful tips for improvement.

The book was realized during my year at the Center for Advanced Study for Behavioral Sciences in Palo Alto, California, where the company of a strikingly diverse group of fellows and the climate created by Claude Steele, the director, provided a wonderful setting for its completion. The fellows' enthusiastic reception to my initial presentation of chapter 2 was instrumental in developing a book geared toward the general reader. I am grateful to David Kreps, the senior associate dean, and Robert Joss, dean of the Graduate School of Business, for supporting my visit at the center. Tim Sullivan, an energetic and creative editor at Princeton University Press, was a joy to work with, as was Seth Ditchik. My wife, Sadhna Diwan, has taught me more about collective action than she cares to remember through her own activism. She also encouraged the book project and read each chapter; some of the chapter titles and the title of the book are based on her astute suggestions. So it is to her I dedicate this book with love and gratitude.

Stanford, CA
September 2007

Market Rebels

1

From the Invisible Hand to Joined Hands

But for the personal computing movement, there would be no Apple. Nearly all of the technical aspects associated with personal computing—small computers, microprocessors, keyboard-based interfaces, individual usability—were available in 1972. As early as 1969, Honeywell had released the H316 "Kitchen Computer" priced at $10,600 in the Neiman Marcus catalog, and in 1971 John Blankenbaker had introduced the Kenbak-1 priced at $750 and Steve Wozniak and Bill Fernandez had built their Cream Soda Computer—so named because they drank Cragmont cream soda as they built the computer with chips discarded by local semiconductor companies.

But the idea of using computers as personalized tools that augmented the autonomy of individuals only took root because of the efforts of hobbyists and engineers.[1] According to some, the first shot of the personal computing movement was in 1966 when Steven Gray founded the Amateur Computing Society and published a newsletter for hobbyists, which became a model for hobbyist clubs around the country. At that time, large firms such as IBM or DEC were dedicated to a centralized conception of computing in which the mainframe was tended by a priesthood of managers, engineers, and operators who prevented users from touching and working with the computer. Their focus effectively blinkered them to the other possibilities—that fans and tinkerers *should* have access and that they could in fact make a bundle by serving that market. As one historian of computing noted, "The most rigid rule was that no one should be able to touch or tamper with the machine itself. This, of course, was what these people (fans) were dying to do more than anything in the world, and the restrictions drove them mad."[2]

The *People's Computer Company,* a bi-monthly newsletter, was started in 1972 and claimed that "computers are mostly used to control people instead of to *free* them . . . it is time to change that."[3] The *People's Computer Company* soon had a circulation of 8,000 and later featured a comic strip built around the characters F-Man and Billy Basic, parodying the programming language Fortran and Bill Gates. In 1974 Ted Nelson, who had founded Project Xanadu in 1960 with the goal of creating a computer network with a simple user interface, published his book *Computer Lib/Dream Machines,* an evangelical appeal for computing to be made available to all without complications or servility. Soon, the first kit-computer, the Altair, priced at $397, was featured on the cover of the January 1975 issue of *Popular Electronics.* Later, the *People's Computer Company*'s cover showcased the Altair.

A few months later, in March 1975, two members of the People's Computer Company, Gordon French and Fred Moore, founded the Homebrew Computer Club in Menlo Park, California. Those who assembled were fans or hobbyists who made personal computers for personal consumption on a small scale, and the name Homebrew symbolized their approach—to go out and claim technology and adjust its recipe to meet personal needs. It also represented a sense of camaraderie, a chance to gripe and to bask in friends' acclaim, an opportunity to pool knowledge, to share techniques and know-how. The Homebrew Computer Club allowed the enthusiasts to express themselves, to be who they really were. The first meeting attracted other enthusiasts, and in December 1975 Mountain View saw the establishment of the first Byte shop to sell components to hobbyists. Soon, other Homebrew clubs were started elsewhere in the United States, quickly becoming spawning grounds for inventors and for founders of companies such as Apple, as well as for developers of programs and games. This groundswell finally woke up IBM and other manufacturers, establishing the market for personal computers and making it possible for larger firms to then enter the market.

■

But for the deaf rights movement, cochlear implants could have transformed the world for deaf children under the age of five. Unlike other hearing aids that amplify sound, the cochlear implant stimulates auditory nerves. Sometimes referred to as the "bionic ear," the implant was thought of by its makers as a cure for deafness because children who used it could easily acquire language skills and become assimilated into society. Thus, from their point of view, the bionic ear was a device that could transform a deaf person from disabled to "normal."

Manufacturers of cochlear implants were surprised when the National Association of the Deaf spearheaded a social movement challenging the depiction of the deaf as disabled and instead arguing that the deaf were a minority culture with a distinct identity and language that was being oppressed by the majority "hearing culture." A telling illustration of the deaf community's perspective on cochlear implants was a cartoon in *Silent News*, the national deaf newspaper, by Bruce Hanson, which showed a jackboot labeled "Hearing" crushing small figures named "Deaf." Deaf activists painted the cochlear implant as a tool of cultural genocide, an innovation that presaged the loss of sign language and the destruction of the deaf community if cochlear implants were used in young deaf children. In France, for example, a deaf coalition called Sourds en Colere (Deaf Anger) organized demonstrations against doctors who promoted cochlear implants. In the United States, deaf pride activists lobbied state legislatures, filed suits for the protection of the rights of deaf parents, and pushed for the regulation and restriction of cochlear implants for young children.

■

What's going on in these two examples? What could the personal computer revolution and the marketing failure of the cochlear implant have to do with one another? Both cases feature radical business innovation that takes the shape of new technologies that challenge existing interests, norms, and values because they disrupt an existing technological trajectory and introduce a brand-new set of performance features to consumers. Most important, radical innovations transform social practices and social relationships and, hence, challenge existing norms and presuppositions. If the personal computer *personalized* computing, the bionic ear signaled the end of sign language and the culture built around it.[4]

In both cases, market rebels, that is, activists who challenged the status quo, played an important role. Hobbyists rebelling against centralized computing and deaf rights champions challenging business firms sparked organized collective endeavors to protect a sense of self—an identity. Radical innovations such as the hybrid car by Toyota succeeded in part because market rebels spearheading the environmental movement had paved the way by arousing collective enthusiasm for "green" causes among consumers and regulators. By contrast, radical innovations such as the Segway floundered because they overlooked the social and cultural mobilization of their targeted consumers by activists.

Despite this, academics who address the question of how markets work, mostly economists and sociologists, have glossed over the role of social movements in shaping radical innovation in markets.[5] Since Adam Smith wrote his treatises in the late eighteenth century, economists have tended to see markets as guided by an invisible hand, wherein individuals acting in their self-interest enhance collective welfare even if it is not their intention to do so. In this focus, economists have largely neglected to understand how the *joined hands* of activists and their recruits make or break radical innovation in markets. Ironically, although sociologists have pioneered the study of social movements, the bulk of their research concerns social movements directed against the state or movements designed to change popular culture, such as large-scale revolutions, civil rights movements, and the women's movement. For the most part, students of technological innovations have treated them as shocks to a market rather than as the outcomes of collective action.[6]

■ Shaping the Market

Scholars and practitioners of marketing innovations have treated the diffusion of innovations as an epidemic whereby contact with a prior adopter induces others to adopt the innovation. However, they often overlook the distinction between simple contagion and complex contagions. Diseases usually entail simple contagion in which *multiple exposures to a single source* is sufficient to spread the disease. For incremental innovations where the costs of adoption are low, simple contagions suffice. By contrast, for radical innovations where the costs of adoption are high because adopters have to topple existing conventions, complex contagions featuring *exposure to multiple sources* are a prerequisite.[7]

The metaphor of an epidemic is an attractive device to use to understand the spread of an innovation, but it relies on the logic of spontaneous combustion—you catch fire when a neighbor catches fire—yet says little about how the neighbor catches fire in the first place. The problem is all the more acute in the case of complex contagions where we need to understand how the multiple sources caught fire. This is where market rebels play a crucial role.

How do the joined hands of market rebels and their recruits shape radical innovation in markets? Political scientists suggest that market rebels, or activists, supply information about firms to consumers through attention-grabbing tactics ranging from picket lines and strikes to certifying the producers who meet their criteria (for instance, the caption "dolphin safe" on tuna cans).[8] Market rebels forsake public politics for private politics, targeting individual firms by organizing campaigns that promise a reward if the firm complies or threaten a penalty if it does not. In response, firms build their reputations to deter counterattacks.[9]

This is undoubtedly true. But the political science perspective treats market rebels as critics who supply *information* while overlooking how they mobilize collective action by harnessing the power of identity. Picketing and other signals are important, but the Homebrewers wanted to do more than force IBM to change; they wanted to play and engage. The deaf rights community sought to do more than just picket cochlear implant makers; they wanted to defend deaf culture.

Social movements are collective endeavors to initiate social change, and they arise to reshape markets when normal incentives are inadequate and when actors are excluded from conventional channels of redress to address social costs.[10] The challenge for market rebels becomes how to forge a collective identity and mobilize support by articulating a *hot cause* that arouses emotion and creates a community of members, and relying on *cool mobilization* that signals the identity of community members and sustains their commitment.

The metaphors of heating up and refreezing are central to the ideas of Kurt Lewin, a psychologist who conceived of social change as a three-step process: unfreezing group life from its current level, moving it to a new level, and refreezing group life at the new level to prevent backsliding.[11] Activists face what can be called a "B2B" dilemma: should one concentrate on changing beliefs first or modifying behavior first? Are beliefs the cause of behavior or their consequence?

But this preoccupation with beliefs or behaviors undercuts the role of emotions and the processes of heating and cooling in social change. Indeed, emotions underlie beliefs and behaviors. A number of social psychological studies highlight "hot cognition"—cognitive cues trigger feelings, and in turn, feelings activate stored knowledge and memories.[12] Other studies reveal that behaviors are "emotional accomplishments"—thus Arlie Hochschild, a sociologist at the University of California–Berkeley, argues that feeling rules or norms govern the expression of behavior in service settings, and that the same behavior is reconstituted when it is infused with different feelings.[13]

How do emotions bridge the belief-versus-behavior debate? How do they trigger social change? The neglect of emotions in social change is all the more surprising given that activists who seek to mobilize the marginal and the powerless largely rely on emotions. *Hot causes* promote unfreezing and changing because they emit new cues that awaken new feelings that interact with the emotions tied to old but relevant beliefs and induce dissonance. *Cool mobilization* contributes to moving and refreezing because it promotes new behaviors, creating new social experiences and affirming new concepts, identities, and commitments. Hot causes and cool mobilization overcome the "B2B" dilemma; hot causes mobilize passions and engender new beliefs, and cool mobilization triggers new behavior and allows new beliefs to develop. Together, they foster the development of new identities and the defense of old ones.

In the personal computing movement, the hot cause was the tyranny of the central computer; the cool sources of mobilization were hobbyist clubs and, arguably, the personal computer itself. Early rebels took computers to the streets by establishing the first community bulletin board with remote terminals placed in a small shopping area where individuals could come in and operate the terminals and do anything they wanted. These early bulletin boards enabled them to recruit others to the hobbyist clubs and, in turn, spawn more rebels who experimented with making computers from kits. In the deaf rights movement, the hot cause was the cochlear implant—billed as a tool of genocide. The cool mobilization was through deaf rights groups that used unconventional techniques to arouse public interest. Consider one episode of the deaf rights movement in France that was emblematic of the hot cause and cool solution. On October 16, 1996, Sourds en Colere organized a demonstration in the medical university of Lyon, which was hosting a conference on cochlear implants. The demonstrators mobilized six hundred people by placing posters where deaf people were likely to see them (schools, deaf organizations), disrupted the conference and gained television coverage at noontime, performed mime skits depicting rapacious doctors performing operations on blood-covered children, and watched a young man hammer the microphone used in a cochlear implant. These techniques of cool mobilization were improvisational, experimental, and insurgent methods of disavowing the cochlear implant and affirming one's own deaf identity.

■ Hot Causes

The challenge for activists is to arouse to action individuals who are usually busy, distracted, uninvolved, or apparently powerless. Hot causes permit arousal because they frame reality. How specifically do hot causes arouse emotions? Social psychologists John Jost and Mahzarin Banaji contend that powerless individuals perpetuate their situation through a number of system-justifying myths that reinforce inertia; they may see their subordinated position as being legitimate, believe that higher status groups are more desirable, and accept their fate as inevitable, or subscribe to widely shared stereotypes.[14] How are the powerless awakened? How are the disinterested motivated to take action? My Stanford colleagues Deb Gruenfeld and Lara Tiedens have shown in separate studies that emotions of power and powerlessness activate different behaviors: feelings of high power trigger assertive and confident behaviors, whereas feelings of powerlessness exacerbate withdrawal behaviors. Positive feelings such as pride and negative feelings such as anger can trigger a high sense of power.[15]

So hot causes arouse pride or anger and impel individuals to invest time and energy. A useful refinement is provided by the sociologist James Jasper, who distinguishes between reciprocal emotions and shared emotions.[16] Reciprocal emotions consist of the feelings of movement participants for each other, such as friendship and solidarity. Shared emotions are also held by movement members but the object is *outside* the movement—an external threat or enemy. Both reciprocal and shared emotions reinforce each other. Alternately, shared feelings of respect for an external group such as customers create reciprocal feelings of pride. A classic example is the quality movement that transformed the American automobile industry—this example is classic because one would expect quality improvements to be undertaken by firms because of normal profit incentives. However, American automobile producers overlooked quality and initially disregarded Japanese innovations concerning quality circles. It was only after a threat was named—the death of the American automobile industry—that quality activists were able to mobilize support for quality institutes and initiatives. The establishment of the Baldrige Award also provided encouragement to the quality movement and led to the restoration of pride in American manufacturing. Thus, hot causes are effective at fostering deep shared and reciprocal emotions when they fit with everyday life experiences of participants and resonate with deeply held cultural narratives.

■ Cool Mobilization

If words are important for the transfer of ideas, nonverbal cues are essential to the transfer of feelings. A number of studies have demonstrated that the diffusion of emotion requires face-to-face contact. It involves little deliberate and purposive processing of information and instead occurs automatically.[17] Like hot causes, cool mobilization activates emotion and enables the formation of new identities, but it does so by engaging audiences in new behaviors and new experiences that are improvisational and insurgent.

The origins of "cool" can be traced to jazz musicians who were revolting against the legacy of Louis Armstrong, who along with his band had become synonymous with "hot jazz." Rebels such as Charlie Parker, Dizzy Gillespie, and Miles Davis saw themselves as belonging to a distinct social group—they spoke slang, wore Ivy League clothing, and, according to some observers, used technical chord progressions to exclude unwanted outsiders. Later, Marshall McLuhan, the media theorist, distinguished between hot media and cool media on the basis of their definition and the extent to which they elicited participation.[18] Hot media like radio and newspaper engage one sense (hearing or vision) and are highly defined and so require little involvement. By contrast, cool media like television engage multiple senses and the involvement of an audience because they are not as highly defined. In this book, I use the term "cool" to capture the insurgent and improvisational dimension in jazz, as well as the low-definition and high-involvement experiences mentioned by McLuhan.

The key in cool mobilization is to engage audiences through collective experiences that generate *communities of feeling,* in which audience members don't just have their emotions aroused but encounter what literary critic Raymond Williams has called *social experiences in solution,* where participants actively *live* meanings and values associated with a social movement.[19] Consider the recycling movement, which seeks to promote sustainable use of resources and rests on the daily ritual of carefully segregating glass, plastic, and paper so that they can be put to later use. Often, these experiences are sustained by social networks that connect participants, or other formal and informal social structures that amplify the initial emotion responsible for joining the movement and strengthen feelings of solidarity. Social experiences in solution arouse feelings of pride and happiness, and, above all, can create a shock of self-discovery as members realize new capacities. In the personal computing movement, for instance, Homebrewing clubs linked hobbyists into a community and made them into both builders and users of personal computers.

Together, then, hot causes and cool solutions power collective action, and collective action creates or constrains markets. Hot causes intensify emotions and trigger new beliefs. Cool mobilization also evokes emotion, but by engaging participants in new collective experiences that transform beliefs. Hot causes are highly defined, and their definition gives them emotional resonance. Cool mobilization has lower definition and requires conscious participation—indeed, participants have to "fill out" the experience through their actions and experimentation. Both underlie the formation of new identities.

As a final introductory example, consider the Slow Food movement—a collective endeavor seeking to defend traditional culture and cuisine that arose in Italy. The hot cause was fast food and its stultifying homogeneity and unhealthiness. The cool mobilization was "slow food"—the communal enjoyment of locally available cuisines. The movement started with a "lightning rod" issue—the establishment of a McDonald's near the Spanish Steps in Rome—that instantly crystallized the movement's grievances. Carlo Petrini, a leader of the gastronomical branch of ARCI (a national network of social clubs tied to the Italian Communist Party), and his associates organized a cool experience that mobilized the interest and commitment of the audience—a sit-in and pasta-eating contest that rewarded the slowest eater. Their protest action proclaimed that Rome was about "slow food" and local and seasonal cuisine, not "fast food." The event soon blossomed into a movement, helped by the growth of local associations of volunteers who became champions of local cuisines, ingredients, and traditions (the *convivia*). In turn, the growth of *convivia* led to the revival of *osteria*, traditional Italian restaurants that used authentic ingredients and prepared traditional food. In short, the hot cause was "McDomination" concretized by a lightning-rod issue that aroused anger against chains and feelings of solidarity among activists. The cool mobilization hinged on the celebration of local cuisines and the reawakening of local identities. Since its origins, the Slow Food movement has successfully spread from Italy to other Western European countries, as well as to the United States.

■ **Invitation**

Social movements are a double-edged sword: they create new identities and underlie the emergence of new markets, new niches in mature markets, and new styles in markets for creative arts, but at the same time they can arise to protect besieged identities and curtail markets by pushing for new laws, thwarting technological change, and limiting executive discretion. One study shows that media coverage of protests targeting companies reduced stock prices by an average of 0.4 percent to 1 percent.[20]

The joined hands of market rebels make or break radical innovations by exploiting hot causes and cool solutions in many of the markets that affect our daily life. We drive cars, drink beer, patronize restaurants, frequent retail stores, rely on medicines, and purchase stocks—and, as we'll see in later chapters, all of these markets have been shaped by social movements.

Chapter 2 undermines a popular conception that Henry Ford created the automobile industry by showing how automobile clubs transformed the car from a devilish contraption into a cultural necessity. The car was a topic of hot debate, and automobile clubs whose members were early adopters of the automobile rebelled against convention and mobilized support for the car by organizing reliability races, which served as tests that told consumers that cars were viable. The case of the car provides potential clues to the failure of new product innovations such as the Segway.

Chapter 3 tackles a puzzle in economic theory: how is new entry possible in an industry with excessive concentration? The United States has more independently owned breweries than does Germany, which has much lower levels of concentration. The microbrewing rebellion was driven by a hot cause—the tasteless beer made by industrial beer manufacturers—and sustained through cool mobilization— brewpubs that made beer on a small scale with artisanal techniques and traditional materials, making it possible for a new niche to be created in a mature market.

In markets for creative arts, the conditions of production inhibit radical technological change because the work of the performer is an end in itself. If this is true, how does disruptive technological change lead to new products and new processes? Chapter 4 chronicles how the nouvelle cuisine movement was powered by a hot cause—the rigid orthodoxy of classical cuisine—and a cool mobilization—the chef as an inventor and improviser, thereby leading to a technological change in a market for creative arts.

Chapter 5 asks how governance innovations that radically redistribute power in markets become accepted and spread across countries. It looks at how the investor rights movement emerged in the United States and promoted new procedures to set compensation of CEOs and elect directors that sharply reduced the discretion of managers, then spread to Germany—a country with a very different capital market structure than that of the United States.

In dramatic contrast, the next two chapters highlight how market rebels exploit collective action to impede business innovation markets. Chapter 6 explores how social movements can curtail the entry of a technologically superior alternative into existing markets. It studies the popular upsurge against retail chain stores in America during the period starting in the 1920s when chains like A&P and Montgomery Ward proliferated across the country and transformed the retail sector. It elaborates how the anti–chain store movement sought to protect mom-and-pop stores from the advance of large chain stores in the retail sphere in the 1920s by pressuring state legislatures to enact hostile tax laws in the United States and describes the counterattack by chain stores.

Chapter 7 asks how rebels in the "streets" get their ideas into boardroom "suites" and shape the decision making of top managers of large firms. It spells out how anti-biotechnology activists prevented large German pharmaceutical firms from commercializing their knowledge by arousing fears of Nazi-style eugenics, creating regulatory uncertainty that undermined investment calculations, and impugning the identities of scientists. Chapter 8 discusses the implications for constructing hot causes and developing cool solutions for managers.

Market rebels enable and constrain radical business innovation in markets and, therefore, represent a potential opportunity and threat for organizations. This book suggests how to stop thinking like bureaucrats and how to start thinking like insurgents.

"You Can't Get People to Sit on an Explosion!"
The Cultural Acceptance of the Car in America

Consider the electric car. In 1990, California was the first state to issue a "Zero Emissions Vehicle" mandate and virtually ordered automakers to produce electric cars as a growing percentage of their business if they wanted to participate in the market in California. General Motors launched the EV-1 in 1996, and Toyota introduced the RAV4 EV, which plugged into wall outlets and could travel for eighty miles or so before needing a recharge.

Automakers, as the trenchant documentary *Who Killed the Electric Car?* shows, were, at best, half-hearted in their commitment to the electric car and, at worst, fiercely lobbied against the mandate because of their preexisting investment in the gasoline-powered car. Instead of selling electric cars, they leased them to customers, made very few cars and kept customers on the waiting list, used regular lead-acid batteries, and eventually withdrew their products from the market in 2001. A poignant moment in the documentary is when the director, Chris Paine, shows dozens of EV-1 cars crushed and put on flatbed trucks in General Motors' test facility in Arizona while a public relations executive asserted that the company would recycle the electric fleet. Oil companies and the Bush administration also assisted the automaker lobby, and despite the endorsement of celebrities like Tom Hanks and Mel Gibson, the electric car industry failed to take off. Both auto and oil producers were hostile to the electric car, and normal incentives to innovate were inadequate to convince new producers to enter the market. But a principal cause of the electric car's failure was the disinterest of the Californian consumer. Only a social movement powered by rebels dedicated to the electric car, framing it as a solution to the hot causes of oil dependence and global warming, and mobilizing consumer interest through cool techniques, could have saved the electric car. Had it taken off in California, a bellwether state, the electric car industry might well have found a firm footing throughout the United States.

The failure of the electric car to capture consumer interest stands in stark contrast to the success of the gasoline-powered car in early twentieth-century America. If the electric car was undermined by vested interests, the gasoline-powered car, at the inception of the automobile industry in 1895, was poorly understood, notoriously unreliable, and reviled by anti-speeding vigilante organizations.[1] There was no semantic agreement on what a car was—other than the fact that it was not drawn by a horse. Commentators variously referred to it as the "velocipede," "motocycle," "locomobile," "electric runabout," "electric buggy," "horseless carriage," "automobile," and "quadricycle." More important, observers found it hard to comprehend and make sense of the automobile. Producers themselves were somewhat confused: many vehicles were designed with whip sockets and harness hitches, relics of their manufacturers' main line of work—making horse-drawn buggies—and testaments to the unreliability of the car. A producer who went on to make electric cars, Colonel Albert Pope, could not fathom why anyone would use gas- and steam-powered cars, asserting, "You can't get people to sit on an explosion."[2] The car was also referred to as a "devilish contraption," and a lawmaker in Massachusetts suggested that motorists fire Roman candles at approaching horse-drawn carriages to warn them of the arrival of the car. In short, the automobile was a topic of heated controversy.

Yet by 1912, doubts about the car were firmly dispelled, and it was no longer a dubious novelty but an integral part of American culture. As early as 1906, Frank Munsey noted that the "uncertain period of the automobile is now past. It is no longer a theme for jokers and rarely do we hear the derisive expression 'Get a horse.'"[3] By 1909, Charles Duryea remarked that the "novelty of the automobile has largely worn off."[4] The automobile was an unquestioned element of American society, and by 1913 Henry Ford installed the moving assembly line in Highland Park, Michigan, to mass produce the Model T.

How did the automobile gain cultural acceptance and legitimacy? How was its identity transformed from a "devilish contraption" to a safe and reliable mode of individualized transportation? How did it become embedded in the prevalent culture? New industries can grow only when they are understood, accepted, and taken for granted by prospective consumers, financiers, employees, entrepreneurs, and governmental authorities—when they gain what sociologists refer to as legitimacy.[5] Laws licensing the new technology and regularizing its use had to be in place too: laws licensing drivers and mandating speed limits defused opposition to the car from anti-speed vigilante organizations. In turn, when an industry has legitimacy, it is also likely to attract complementary assets. So roads had to be built for cars rather than horseless carriages, which attracted new producers.

Popular accounts of new industries eulogize visionary entrepreneurs as the harbingers of legitimacy for radically new technologies. Thus Henry Ford, for example, is widely thought of as the man who established the automobile industry. But Ford only installed the moving assembly line after the car became taken for granted, and he benefited from laws licensing drivers and mandating speed limits. In sharp contrast, economic theory says that the pioneers of an industry incur the cost of legitimating the new industry: they establish a trade association, lobby governments, and establish supply and distribution networks. They bear these costs since they can gain a large share of the market. To be sure, some new industries are established through collective action by pioneering producers. But trade associations may come asunder due to coordination costs because agreements may be hard to negotiate as each party seeks to gain positional advantage. Indeed, in the automobile industry, early attempts to form trade associations fragmented because of internecine warfare. Normal incentives were inadequate as auto companies issued misleading advertisements and damaged the image of the car.

Alexis de Tocqueville described America as a society of joiners and associations, observing, "In no other country in the world has the principle of association been more successfully used or applied toward a greater multitude of objects than in America."[6] In the case of the automobile, a social movement powered by automobile clubs composed of car enthusiasts played a central role in legitimating the automobile and presenting it as a modern solution to the problem of transportation. These enthusiasts were rebels who flouted convention and abandoned the horse-drawn carriage for the automobile, and sought to popularize its use.

Below, I draw on my prior research using data gleaned from the remarkable journal *The Horseless Age*—a publication that started in 1895 and was the forerunner of the *Automotive News*—and other sources to show how the automobile was a hot cause surrounded by controversy and how it became accepted because automobile clubs exploited a cool technique of mobilization—the reliability contest. Auto clubs were social movement organizations that not only worked with state governments to draft laws licensing cars and mandating speed limits but also framed the car as reliable and safe by organizing reliability contests. In these contests, cars were pitted against one another and evaluated in endurance, hill-climbing, and fuel-economy runs. Endurance contests were different from speed contests, which featured cars that were specially designed to shatter speed records. Reliability contests were framing devices that blended the practice of racing with the logic of product testing. Each contest was widely viewed as a test that told audiences that the automobile was reliable. The first reliability contest was in 1895, and by 1912 reliability contests were discontinued because organizers recognized that the automobile was no longer an artifact but a social fact. Soon thereafter, Henry Ford initiated the mass production of cars.

■ **The Early Automobile as a Hot Cause**

The early American automobile industry constituted a radical departure from its precursor, the horse carriage industry. Unlike the horse carriage industry, which relied on animal power, automobile firms used steam, gasoline, and electric power to provide customers with horseless carriages. Horse carriage firms were one-man operations, but early automobile firms were assemblers who put together components supplied by other companies.[7] Above all, the automobile was a radical invention that promised to transform the experience of transportation. The automobile was a *hot cause.*

At the dawn of the automobile industry, the car was an unfamiliar product and incomprehensible to many observers. The only point of agreement about the automobile was that it could not be powered by animals. Otherwise, anything went. Consumers debated the source of power, the number of cylinders, the systems of steering and control, and the mode of stopping—all were topics of considerable controversy. Consumers were hesitant to purchase cars because they could not evaluate their post-purchase quality.

Producers did not understand the automobile either. Hiram Maxim, a pioneer of the industry, wrote that he was "blissfully ignorant that others were working with might and main . . . on road vehicles."[8] Cars were also unreliable; it was not unusual for drivers to break their bones when they started their gasoline-powered car with a handle. The problem was complicated by the fact that many of the early manufacturers were only remotely connected to making cars. For example, the Smith Automobile Company of Topeka,

Kansas, was in the business of making hernia trusses before (and after) taking up automobile manufacturing. Misleading advertisements issued by some firms evoked editorials against the "endless amount of nonsense being published in the public press."[9]

Since the automobile threatened to displace the horse-drawn carriage, it could have triggered opposition from manufacturers of horse-drawn carriages, livery stable owners, and horse-drawn vehicle driver associations. But opposition by existing manufacturers of carriages was minimal. Instead, prominent manufacturers of horse-drawn carriages such as Studebaker, Flint Wagon, Standard Wheel Company, and Mitchell Wagon Company themselves entered the automobile industry and began to produce motor cars. Enterprising owners of livery stables also switched to opening garages or to starting car rental services.

By contrast, vigilantes opposed to speed were the principal source of opposition to users of cars. The most aggressive anti-speed organizations, such as the Long Island Highway Protective Society, described speeders as "scorchers" and resorted to illegal tactics such as puncturing the tires of speeding cars and in some cases even riddling tires with bullets. Opposition to speed existed in rural areas during the touring season when speeding automobilists threatened livestock and horse-drawn traffic, and raised dust that damaged crops.[10] The Farmer's Anti-automobile Society of Pennsylvania demanded, "Automobiles traveling on country roads at night must send up a rocket every mile, then wait ten minutes for the road to clear. If a driver sees a team of horses, he is to pull to one side of the road and cover his machine with a blanket or dust cover that has been painted to blend into the scenery. In the event that a horse refuses to pass a car on the road, the owner must take his car apart and conceal the parts in the bushes."[11] Some farming communities (as in Rochester, Minnesota) plowed roads to make them unusable by cars, and local businessmen in some counties were threatened with boycotts by farmers should they buy motor cars.

Firms within the new industry could not successfully band together to legitimate the automobile. In the first four years, no trade associations existed to advance the cause of the automobile. The National Association of Automobile Manufacturers was established only in 1900 in a bid to assure product quality, but it was superseded by the Association of Licensed Automobile Manufacturers (ALAM) in 1903. ALAM was a trade association formed to license the Selden patent—George Selden of Rochester, New York, had patented a "Road Engine" and required manufacturers to license his technology—and was set up ostensibly to prevent "incursion of piratical hordes who . . . desire to flood the market with trashy machines."[12] But the Selden patent was widely disregarded and, due to internal divisions, ALAM was unable to secure quality by enforcing its threat of litigation. A rival association called the American Motor Car Manufacturer's Association (AMCMA) was established in 1905 and proved to be an ineffective mechanism of collective action. Both trade associations disintegrated between 1909 and 1911 as a result of legal battles. Neither cartel could deter defection or prevent cheating, and both were overwhelmed by the rate of entry of new firms. Since there were no effective trade associations and the federal government was inactive, it was not possible to formulate a national license and registration policy to defuse opposition to the car from anti-speeding interests.

Professional societies did not exert a decisive influence on the legitimacy of the automobile industry and gained strength only after the car had become culturally accepted in America as a necessity of modern life. The Society of Automobile Engineers (SAE) began in 1905 with a small group of journalists and automobile engineers, and only established a standards committee by 1910, which diagnosed the lack of intercompany standardization of components as a major cause of production problems and expenses. A program of standard setting was initiated that eventually resulted (in 1921) in the formation of 224 standards.

Professionals also did not play an important role in training personnel. In 1905, the New York School of Automobile Engineers was established by a professor of engineering from Columbia, and a handful of other affiliates arose in a few large cities to disseminate mechanical expertise relevant to the automobile. However, the professionalization of automobile engineering really began when the SAE began a large training effort after 1912—by then the car was established in American culture.

In other new industries, large business-to-business customers such as the military might have had substantial effects on the legitimacy of the automobile. The governments of France, Germany, and England had discerned the military potential of the automobile and offered subsidies for the development of military vehicles, which inhibited the manufacture of light cars. By contrast, in the United States the War Department only began to acquire specialized automobiles in 1909. Similarly, the post office, although more alert than the War Department, experimented with the use of motor vehicles to collect mail beginning in 1896, and even started subcontracting mail collection to private entrepreneurs in a series of tests from 1901 to 1906. The post office made a substantial commitment to the purchase of motor vehicles in New York City in 1909 and after that encouraged the use of automobiles for free rural delivery. Thus, the federal government, despite its potential to influence the market through buyers such as the War Department or the post office, exercised little influence on the rise of the automobile industry in the United States.[13]

It was under these circumstances that the "automobile club became the most important champion of the diffusion of the automobile in the United States. Voluntary associations of motorists propagandized to encourage a favorable image of the automobile and automobilists."[14] Local clubs of motorcar enthusiasts were organized in cities and towns, and by 1901 twenty-two local clubs had mushroomed in different cities from Boston to Newark and Chicago. By 1904, it was "as difficult to find a number of motorists who have not formed a club, as it is to find an individual motorist who is not a member of some such body."[15]

As with the rise of the bicycle in America, where bicycle clubs formed by cycling enthusiasts played a more important role in establishing the bicycle as a source of health than did individual producers who bankrolled campaigns to advertise the bicycle as a valued product,[16] committed activists tend to be more effective when they are formally organized. Social movement organizations like automobile clubs make it easier for activists to disseminate information, gain attention, and recruit other activists. Such organizations promote face-to-face communication and enable activists to develop a sense of collective identity. In turn, close contact facilitates the exchange of specialized political knowledge necessary to mobilize a group, enables network formation, and thwarts organized opposition.

Local clubs were voluntary self-help societies designed to share information about cars with a view toward improving quality, shielding car owners from legal harassment, and promoting good roads. For example, the New Jersey Automobile and Motor Club had no clubhouse but devoted much of its attention to the passage of car laws. Auto clubs were social clubs mainly composed of doctors, who were the first to use the automobile in large numbers, other professionals, and members of the local elite, and were neither sponsored nor financed by car manufacturers. The American Automobile Association (AAA) began as an association of local clubs and, after some early disagreements with the New York clubs, emerged as the primary representative of car owners in America. By 1910, there were 225 local clubs affiliated with AAA.

Some clubs organized tours for underprivileged children to dissuade them from throwing stones at passing cars in places such as Chicago and New York. Initially, the National Association of Automobile Manufacturers, the abortive trade association, sought to have federal legislation provide a national license, but it made little headway because Congress and the federal government were apathetic toward the automobile until 1909. By contrast, many municipal governments wanted to arrest speeders and insisted that each car should have a numbered tag. Local automobile clubs initially challenged these city ordinances but quickly realized that a maze of municipal regulations could only be checked if there were statewide rules for registering and licensing automobiles. In this context, reliability contests not only made the car familiar to the public but also enabled auto clubs to signal the strength of their constituency and made it easier for them to persuade state authorities to enact laws routinizing the licensing of cars and mandating a speed limit. For example, the Auto Club of Seattle was started as a social club on September 23, 1904, with forty-six members, and one of its first actions was to help draft the first driving law, which the state of Washington adopted on March 8, 1905.

■ Cool Mobilization through Reliability Contests

Auto club members were evangelists who transformed the identity of the automobile from a "devilish contraption" into a safe and reliable means of transportation by organizing reliability contests. They codified rules for reliability races and provided the personnel for scheduling and supervising these contests. As early as 1901, the AAA chapter in New York City formulated a set of racing rules and assisted local auto clubs in scheduling contests.

In 1900 ten automotive enthusiasts founded the Auto Club of Los Angeles and soon sponsored and sanctioned reliability contests in Santa Monica and oval track events at what is now Exposition Park near downtown Los Angeles. Similarly, on March 25, 1903, twelve Vermonters gathered in the Pavilion Hotel in Montpelier to form the Automobile Club of Vermont to "secure rational legislation, rules and regulations governing the use of automobiles, to maintain the lawful rights of owners and users of automobiles, to promote and encourage improvements of the highways of the State and to maintain a social club devoted to automobilism." By 1905 the club had a total of 103 members. It sponsored two "runs" each year that served two purposes: "to enjoy the countryside and to promote the use of the Automobile."[17] The formation of an auto club was a precursor to a reliability run rather than a consequence, and reliability contests increased public interest and, eventually, car ownership and membership in the auto clubs.

Theoretically, auto firms *could* have organized a contest, but they didn't. Ford could have invited anyone to duel their car in endurance runs or hill-climbing runs. However, firms faced two impediments. Firms were unlikely to enter such head-to-head contests and risk being penalized by negative publicity. Moreover, they had little need to do so since auto clubs, impartial third parties, were already organizing contests. Automobile clubs perceived reliability contests as a subtle strategy of promoting the acceptance of the car by the public. For example, some activists organized competitions "with the desire to promote, encourage and stimulate the invention, development and perfection and general adoption of motor vehicles."[18] Club members were typically car-owning enthusiasts who were early users of cars, and club involvement enabled members to construct an identity built around a new consumer role. Since reliability contests were spectacles that aroused public interest, they also boosted membership.

The first reliability contest was the *Times-Herald* race held on Thanksgiving Day in 1895. There were six participants: a Duryea, two Benzes, two electric vehicles, and a Mueller. The race course was from Chicago to Evanston and back, a distance of about fifty miles (eighty kilometers). The wintry road conditions extracted a quick toll: the two electrics dropped out as their batteries died, and the duo of Benz automobiles also broke down. The gasoline-powered Duryea made steady progress, though at a rate of under ten miles per hour, and crossed the finish line after nine hours, winning the first prize of $10,000. The *Chicago Times-Herald* proclaimed, "Persons who are inclined . . . to decry the development of the horseless carriage . . . will be forced . . . to recognize it as an admitted mechanical achievement, highly adapted to some of the most urgent needs of our civilization."[19]

Local automobile clubs quickly jumped into the fray to sponsor reliability contests, and soon newspapers were reduced to the role of covering races rather than organizing them. Reliability runs consisted of hill-climbing, endurance, and, on occasion, fuel-economy runs. These runs featured cars that were likely to be used by ordinary consumers, in contrast to speed contests, which included specialized monstrosities unlikely ever to be bought by consumers. Beach, track, and road races were attempts to test technology rather than publicize the motor vehicle.[20]

Auto clubs were organizers of reliability contests—as the number of clubs increased, the frequency of the contests did as well. Data on all reliability races, compiled from *The Horseless Age*, show that each club increased contests by

11 percent.[21] These races bestowed publicity on the winners and allowed them to build reputations for quality.

Ironically, even Henry Ford needed to win a race in order to achieve the transition from engineer to entrepreneur. The public acclaim that Ford received enabled him to create the Ford Motor Company in 1903. Figure 2.1 shows a celebrated race in 1901 featuring Henry Ford, then an upstart producer, and Alexander Winton, an established producer, with Ford about to pull ahead of Winton. Ford's wife, Clara, later described the scene after Ford took the lead in a letter to her brother, Milton Bryant: "The people went wild. One man threw his hat up and when it came down he stamped on it. Another man had to hit his wife on the head to keep her from going off the handle. She stood up in her seat . . . screamed, 'I'd bet $50 on Ford if I had it.'"

Organizers of automobile clubs borrowed the practice of racing from the bicycle industry, blended it with the nascent logic of testing, and constructed credible claims. Individual contests generated winners who quickly acquired a reputation for reliability, but the contests also strengthened the claim of the automobile as a safe and reliable device. Reliability contests were credible because each race was an event that could be interpreted as evidence of the dependability of cars by the public. Since reliability contests were public spectacles, they were emotionally charged events. Finally, reliability contests had "narrative fidelity" because they combined the logic of testing with the practice of racing and created a compelling story.

Bicycle racing had appeared in 1878, soon after the introduction of the bicycle in America. Early bicycle races

Figure 2.1
Ford versus Winton: the Grosse Pointe Race, 1901. Courtesy
of the Smithsonian Institution, NMAH/Transportation.

were road races that sprang out of cycling tours conducted
by bicycle clubs, and almost every city with pretensions of
being important had a road race. Participants were week-
end cyclists of varying ability and were "handicapped" by
clubs such as the League of American Wheelmen and the
Associated Cycling Clubs. The prize went to the man who
finished first, and newspapers featured extensive coverage
of many races, especially prominent ones such as the Pull-
man Road Race held in Chicago that originated in 1883.
Since it was difficult to tell who was winning a road race,
track races first appeared in 1883. As cycle manufacturers
realized the benefits of the publicity that accrued to
them from winning, they began to attract the best racers,
and such "maker's amateurs" made track racing a contest

among manufacturers.[22] Winning firms then advertised victories as evidence of quality.

Concurrently, a nascent logic of testing was also becoming established with the rise of standards and testing bodies that were extensions of trade associations and professional societies seeking to promulgate common metrics to assist business organizations. In 1894, for instance, an association of insurance underwriters (Underwriters Laboratory) received a charter to certify wires and light fixtures as fire resistant in order to build insurable real estate. Other trade associations established standard nomenclatures and performance specifications in the wool blanket and laundry industries. Materials-testing experts promulgated standards for paint, and electrical engineers developed standards for electrical components for large business enterprises.[23] The testing and standards ideas received encouragement from the state when the National Bureau of Standards was founded in 1901; it soon instituted annual national conferences on weights and measures. The *Journal of Weights and Measures* was established in 1908 for the "benefit of Dealers, Sealers and the Purchasing Public."

Reliability contests aroused public interest and diffused knowledge about the car throughout the American populace. But over time, as they enhanced social proof of the automobile as a reliable and dependable means of transportation, the contests began to wane in frequency. A writer commented about the Glidden Tour, a reliability contest, saying that it had "proved the automobile is now almost foolproof. It has proved that American cars are durable and efficient . . . it has strengthened our belief in the *permanence* of the motor car."[24] The prestigious Glidden Tour saw the number of entrants drop to thirteen in 1909, and after 1912, it was discontinued. Soon, the Ford Motor Company stopped participating in reliability contests because they were deemed unnecessary. After 1912, reliability contests ended, but speed contests continued to flourish because they had become a sport.

In short, then, reliability contests were victims of their own success. Each reliability contest reduced the rate at which subsequent contests were organized by 6 percent. As the number of early reliability contests increased and the automobile became accepted and taken for granted, the rate of occurrence of reliability contests declined precipitously. Thus, reliability contests promoted the acceptance of the car and extinguished the need for club members to schedule subsequent reliability contests.

■ Reliability Contests, Organizational Births, and Failures

Reliability contests were visible mechanisms for consumers, founders, and investors to make sense of the new and unfamiliar technology. They made the car "available" to audiences and created a story that resonated with them. By grounding the new product in well-known popular genres, reliability contests made the car comprehensible and fostered a shared symbolic environment in which participants developed understandings of the car. Frequent demonstration events organized by institutional activists provided social proof of the car's safety and viability. It is likely that reliability contests enhanced the legitimacy of the car, exposed potential entrepreneurs to the car, and induced them to start new organizations.

One way to think about how reliability contests increased entrepreneurial activity is to assess whether they induced potential founders (those who possessed a prototype) to venture forth into the production and sale of cars.[25] Each contest increased the odds of founding by .3 percent—so as the number of contests rose from 1 to 100, the odds of founding rose by 30 percent.

Car enthusiasts in automobile clubs found it easy to blend the material practice of racing with the logic of testing. Each contest told a plausible story about the reliability and safety of the car, thereby lowering the failure rates of all car producers. Just as reliability contests promoted the founding of new firms by quashing doubts about the viability of the car, they were also likely to enhance the firms' survival prospects. For individual producers who won a contest, each win was a cue that could be enlarged into a larger and more plausible story about the firm as a producer of quality cars. On the one hand, general newspapers and the trade press took small cues in the form of individual victories and, in their coverage of the races, developed an account of winning and losing firms. On the other hand, winning firms proclaimed their victories in their advertising campaigns and developed advertising themes to signal distinct identities. After winning some hill-climbing contests, the Peerless Company advertised its car as "a rapid and powerful hill climber." Similarly, Cadillac coined the slogan that "when you buy a Cadillac you buy a round trip." After winning several contests, Buick proclaimed, "Tests tell—Could you ask for more convincing evidence?"[26] Figure 2.2 shows the advertisement of the Columbia Car after it won an endurance record.

As certification mechanisms overseen by consumer interests, reliability competitions created differences in the reputations of organizations and created a status hierarchy in the market. High-status firms benefit from what sociologist Robert K. Merton called the "Matthew effect"—derived from a line from the first book of the New Testament: "For unto everyone that hath shall be given, that he may have abundance; but from him that hath not shall be taken away even that which he hath." The Matthew effect simply means that higher-status actors derive greater rewards than lower-status actors for performing an identical task.[27]

Figure 2.2
Advertisement for the Columbia Car.

Reliability runs created the basis for the Matthew effect. Wins generally prolonged the lives of automobile producers. Each win enhanced the status of the producer and reduced the odds of failure by 34 percent.

Were wins, in general, flukes? If wins were random events, then prior cumulative wins should have had an insignificant effect on the rate of subsequent wins. But in fact each win increased the rate of winning by 20 percent, so the rich stayed rich because past winners tended to accumulate more wins. Quite simply, it could be that high-quality firms won because they made high-quality cars. However, one ought not to leap to this conclusion; firms could increase wins simply by participating in more races. A more realistic interpretation is that firms might have secured their initial win on the basis of luck. Then, having been able to sell more cars, they might have participated in more races to maintain their reputations or even created and entered newer models.

One thing is certain: gasoline-powered cars won more frequently than others. On average, they won reliability contests at more than 4.5 times the rate at which steam- or electric-powered cars won. Electric-powered cars could never climb hills quickly and were limited in their speed. Steam-powered cars had speed and could climb hills, but their popularity was undermined by the crash of the Stanley Steamer—also called the "Flying Teapot"—in 1907 in Ormond Beach, Florida. The debacle spawned many myths and undermined confidence in steam cars. The Stanley Steamer never raced again. One description of the incident is as follows:

> The course of an industry, however—like that of an individual or a nation—is sometimes influenced by isolated incidents. Such an incident occurred in 1907 at Ormond Beach, Florida, where a crowd had gathered to watch the annual automobile speed trials. After a number of gasoline cars had made their runs, none reaching the 100 m.p.h. mark, the Stanley Steamer entry appeared. It was a frail vehicle that

looked like a canoe turned upside down and mounted on spindly wheels. The press of the day had dubbed it "The Flying Teapot."

As the Steamer started its run, it emitted a low whistle that rose to a faint whine, and jetlike vapor flowed from the tail of the car. The head of the driver was a blur as the car passed the 100 m.p.h. mark and surged up to 197 m.p.h. As it was about to touch 200 m.p.h., however, the racer hit a slight bump on the beach. The light car soared for about 100 feet at a height of 10 feet, then crashed to the cement-hard sand in an explosion of steam and flames. The driver was flung clear, badly injured but not dead.[28]

After the 1907 debacle, the Stanley Steamers did not race again, and the steam car was undermined by a multiplicity of urban myths: that its throttles could not be controlled by one man, that the flames shooting from the car could cause explosions, and so forth. The electric car was largely seen as a car for women because it was easy to start and slow, and never captured public imagination like the gas-powered cars that won races.

■ Implications

Thus it was not Henry Ford but automobile clubs that played a central role in promoting the cultural acceptance of the car. The auto clubs provide a striking example of Tocqueville's observation, "As soon as several inhabitants of the United

States conceive an idea that they want to produce in the world, they seek each other out; and when they have found each other, they unite. From then on they are no longer isolated, but a power one sees from afar, whose actions serve as an example; a power that speaks, and to which one listens."[29]

A new industry, as sociologists Michael Hannan, Laszlo Polos, and Glenn Carroll point out, presupposes a new category and a code of conduct.[30] Reliability contests established the car as a cultural category, developed a collective identity for car makers, and produced a de facto code of conduct for automobile firms. As reliability contests became more frequent and the audience was exposed to the car, their doubts and questions about the viability of the car were allayed and the car became integrated into the prevailing landscape. So the establishment of car manufacturers was substantially higher in states with reliability contests. Reliability contests spread knowledge about the automobile, made it into a safe, reliable, and dependable product, and reduced exits. Wins in reliability contests were certificates of dependability that allowed winners to extract greater returns in the former of lowered exit probabilities even if the winners produced the same product as non-winners. Moreover, reliability contests also established the basic technology of car making: gas-powered cars tended to win and survived, and eventually new entrants had to make gasoline-powered cars or face extinction.

The history of the automobile industry also provides one clue to the disappointing record of the Segway. In 2001, the Segway Personal Transporter was launched amid great fanfare; it was widely expected to revolutionize lifestyles, solve the problem of congestion, and reshape the landscape.

Financiers such as John Doerr, the venture capitalist who backed Segway, forecasted it to be the company that reached $1 billion in sales in the shortest time in history. The first Segway was purchased by Steve Wozniak—the inventor of the Apple computer. Segway's inventor, Dean Kamen, forecasted they would be manufacturing ten thousand machines a week. The post office, Federal Express, and others were widely predicted to be large consumers. Unlike other radical innovations, the Segway had a number of advantages: media interest, endorsements of celebrities, an inventor with a track record of success, and nifty technology.

Yet sales were disappointing, and published reports indicate that Segway did not sell more than ten thousand machines during the period 2001–4, let alone ten thousand a week. Its steep price ($5,000 or so) and short-lived batteries are often presented as the causes for its failure.

Apropos of our discussion of the car, though, the Segway disrupted the status quo—indeed, many municipalities enacted laws prohibiting or restricting its use—and to take root and ultimately succeed it had to supplant walking. Consumers simply did not think of it as an appropriate solution to the problem of transport. There was no social movement like the automobiling movement to promote the Segway. To be sure, there is a group of enthusiasts, Segway Enthusiasts America, and individual chapters are slowly being established, which have played some role in lobbying local authorities to withdraw bans on the Segway and license its use on pavements and sidewalks. Segway Festivals have now been launched to popularize its use in new contexts (e.g., Segway Polo and the like). But the Segway movement has neither caught the imagination of the public nor mushroomed across the United States.

Our detailed history of the automobile industry also provides a clue to a puzzle in economic theory—the wide variation in the time that new industries take to gain cultural acceptance. When economists Steven Klepper and Elizabeth Graddy studied forty-six different industries, they found that the average duration from inception to cultural acceptance (which they measured as the peak number of producers) was twenty-nine years with a standard deviation of fifteen years; some industries attained the peak in two years, whereas others took fifty years. What explains such substantial variation in cultural acceptance?[31]

The case of the automobile industry suggests that social movement activity explains such variation when producers cannot coordinate and when normal incentives are absent. The automobile industry started in 1895, and it took fifteen years for it to attain cultural acceptance—at least as measured by the number of producers. (The number of producers reached a peak of three hundred in 1910—just about the time Duryea was saying that the automobile was no longer a devilish contraption but an uncontested feature of modern life.)

The saga of the gasoline-powered car shows that collective action by rebels can be decisive in emerging markets. And it points to another set of questions: Can social movements arise in mature markets? What effects do they have? If so, why? What are their causes and consequences? I turn to these issues in chapter 3 by elaborating how movements create new niches in markets with excessive concentrations of market shares, using the microbrewing movement as an example.

Evange-Ale-ists and the Renaissance
of Microbrewing

An early debate in anthropology hinged on whether the urge to brew beer or to make bread was the impetus for human beings to domesticate wild grains, become sedentary, and organize themselves into communities.[1] Two anthropologists, Solomon Katz and Mary Voigt, argued that beer was the driving force for the domestication of grains and the organization of communities because it provided nutrition and eventually became incorporated into social and religious systems.[2] Indeed, a tablet dated to 1800 BC contains a "Hymn to Ninkasi," which invoked the Sumerian goddess of brewing, and Hammurabi's code, also dating to 1800 BC, prescribes penalties for offenses at beer taverns.

Brewing was the mainstay of local communities and diversity in America and was mainly fueled by immigration from Germany. By the mid-1870s, there were more than four thousand small local breweries in America, and after the repeal of Prohibition more than seven hundred breweries were resurrected. This diversity was whittled away by market concentration—so much so that by the 1980s, the four largest producers accounted for 80 percent of the market share.[3]

Hence, September 26, 1997, was a watershed day in the history of the modern brewing industry in America: the Institute of Brewing Studies announced that the United States exceeded Germany in the number of breweries. In comparison to the 1,234 breweries in Germany, the United States had 1,273 breweries, and of them 1,250 were microbrewers. Compare this to the eight microbreweries that existed in 1980. By 2003, the number of craft brewers had reached 1,492. Why did microbrewers proliferate, especially when the four largest brewers controlled 98 percent of the market share in 2003?

The proliferation of microbrewers violates two tenets of industrial economics: that rising concentration deters entry and that industries transit through a growth phase culminating in peak numbers of producers, a shakeout phase in which the efficient survive, and a concentration phase in which a handful of incumbents gain dominance.[4] The rise of microbrewers suggests that new entry is possible even in the face of excessive concentration of market shares and that industries go through a fourth phase—variety proliferation. It is tempting to ascribe the proliferation of variety to rising consumer affluence, but such explanations founder because they do not account for why established firms do not capitalize on the new market segments.[5]

Sociologist Glenn Carroll suggests that variety proliferation occurs in the face of high concentration because of resource partitioning between large generalist firms and small specialist firms. In the early phase of a population's history, a few organizations exploit resources at the center. As these generalists compete with one another, their number shrinks, and the survivors dominate the center of the market and rely on economies of scale. Such rising concentration frees up resources at the periphery for specialist organizations to cater to new consumer tastes. Large generalists find it difficult to pursue these peripheral opportunities because they have to decentralize and undercut their economies of scale. A number of studies have shown that rising competition among large-scale mass producers (generalists) promotes the births of specialist organizations as a result of resource partitioning in mature industries ranging from newspapers to auditing services.[6]

If so, since those at the periphery possess meager finances and political influence to take on dominant and entrenched players, how do they proliferate? How are resources at the periphery created to be partitioned? How did resource partitioning underlie the proliferation of microbrewers?

Social movements arise in markets when participants feel excluded from conventional channels of redress, deprived of support of the state, or starved of media exposure, or some combination thereof. In such cases, identity movements, informed by a "we feeling," arise to challenge dominant organizations or categories and seek to realize new collective identities by building new organizations that emphasize democracy, participation, and empowerment.[7] Microbreweries and brewpubs were outcroppings of a craft movement powered by beer lovers—whom I call evangeale-ists—discontented with the industrial beer produced by big beer companies.[8] Beer enthusiasts were rebels who constructed a *hot cause* (the atrocious taste of mass-produced beer) and relied on *cool mobilization* (small brewpubs using traditional methods and authentic artisanal techniques that offered distinctive beers and, therefore, added to cultural diversity).

■ The Decline of Brewing Diversity in America, 1870–1980

The four million or so Germans who migrated to the United States in the second half of the nineteenth century brought with them a taste for beer, along with their own beer-making traditions and styles. "Wherever Germans are to be found," wrote William Downard in his study of the Cincinnati brewing industry, "there also you will find beer, the bourgeois democratic beverage that never comes amiss when one can't think of anything else that one specially wants to drink and that goes so well with a cigar."[9] Thoreau suggested that "the tavern will compare favorably with the church" and noted it was the place where sermons took effect.[10] Beer had a distinct identity closely tied to the community: it was a friendly drink, a family drink, a healthy drink, and a national drink as depicted in figure 3.1. As a friendly drink, beer was consumed in beer gardens that proliferated in American cities with the arrival of German immigrants. They were gathering places for the men and women in a community and often featured exotic plants and palm trees.

By the 1880s, there were more than four thousand local breweries making unique local brews. As beer barons like Captain Frederic Pabst, George Ehrens, Adolphus Busch, and Colonel Jacob Ruppert built beer empires, opposition to beer also intensified from temperance activists who were the first generation of market rebels that transformed the beer industry in America.

As early as 1846, Neal Dow collected forty thousand signatures in Maine and forced the legislature to pass a prohibition law, which was strengthened in 1851. The Maine laws be-

Figure 3.1
An old beer label.

came a prototype for similar laws in twelve other states. These laws impeded the establishment of breweries and accelerated the demise of breweries in adjacent states.[11] Brewery managers were outraged by prohibition laws, and one such manager in a Kansas brewery wrote to his relatives in Germany,

> We are doing our best to resist the trickery of these fanatic prohibitionists. Our business has managed to change with the times, and it could turn into a gold mine if it weren't for these insane, restrictive laws here. . . . In our town as also in a few other benevolent places around and about, establishments which serve alcohol are tolerated if they pay a monthly fine

that comes out to about 200 marks a month. Most of these towns are always in debt, so they feel they need this income. That is the only reason drinking establishments are tolerated at all. There is no repeal of this crazy prohibition law in sight. I suspect as soon as I can, I will get out of this business and return to farming.[12]

Prohibition laws waned at the onset of the Civil War, and by 1870 many of these laws were repealed. But temperance forces were already regrouping. As early as 1869, the Prohibition Party was founded and campaigned to ban alcohol in all forms, and the Women's Christian Temperance Union was started in 1874. The Anti-Saloon League was formed in 1893 with one motto, "The saloon must go." These organizations attacked the identity of beer, as well as the beer drinker; beer was no longer a friendly drink but a vice, and the beer drinker was no longer someone who enjoyed fellowship but was instead a slave. The Women's Christian Temperance Union and the Anti-Saloon League relied on pledges to abstain from alcohol, marches on state capitals, and letter-writing campaigns to ban alcohol.

World War I provided temperance forces an opportunity to exploit anti-German sentiment, framing temperance as a patriotic duty. The Anti-Saloon League described beer in Milwaukee as "Kaiserbrew" and defined beer as a German drink that deserved to be abandoned. The leader of the Anti-Saloon League asked why soldiers ought to die overseas fighting Germans and or die from drink made by Germans. Figure 3.2 shows one of the fliers used by the Anti-Saloon

League to drive home the link between patriotism and abstinence, and brewers and disloyalty.

Under this onslaught, beer makers like Anheuser-Busch, who invoked Bavarian patriot Andreas Hofer in their advertising campaigns and described him as a lover of liberty who would not tolerate Prohibition, soon deemphasized their German roots. The temperance forces depicted Prohibition as a necessity of war, a means to ensure that grain was made into bread for the army and not liquor. The brewers pointed out that taxes on liquor contributed more to the war effort than liberty bonds, but this argument failed to gain traction. Temperance societies and the anti-saloon leagues targeted beer, gambling, and prostitution, overcame opposition from brewers, the German-American alliance of immigrants and soldiers returning from World War I, and succeeded in establishing Prohibition from 1920 until 1933.

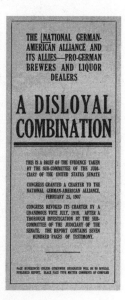

Figure 3.2
Anti-German poster of the Anti-Saloon League. Westerville Public Library.

Before Prohibition, 1,100 breweries were in operation, but many turned to the manufacture of cereal beverages. By September 1923, three years into Prohibition, there were 500 cereal beverage plants in operation in the United States—just three could have fulfilled the nation's need for cereal beverages. Some breweries transformed themselves into makers of "soft" drinks. Thus, Anheuser-Busch made Malt-Nutrine, an

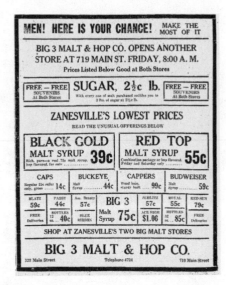

Figure 3.3
An advertisement
for malt syrup during
Prohibition.

"invigorating and sedative tonic," Car-cho, a chocolate soda, and even imitation grape syrup. An effort to co-opt physicians and advocate the cause of "medical beer" as a health drink fizzled.

Even if Prohibition sounded the death knell of the brewing industry, it also led to the hobby of home brewing (*heimgemacht* in German).[13] Malt syrup was a staple for home-brewed beer, and former brewers and stores advertised malt syrup to men. Figure 3.3 shows an old advertisement for malt syrup, bottle caps, and other materials, which appeared in the Zanesville *Signal* on September 15, 1928, touting the names of beers such as Schlitz and Blue Ribbon.

Since making a cereal beverage involved making real beer and then removing the alcohol, makers of cereal beverages had the opportunity to take this beer and sell it to

Table 3.1

Concentration of Market Shares in the Brewing Industry, 1947–81

Year	Share of Five Largest Firms (%)	Share of Ten Largest Firms (%)
1947	19.0	28.2
1954	24.9	38.3
1958	28.5	45.2
1964	39.0	58.2
1968	47.6	63.2
1974	64.0	80.8
1978	74.3	92.3
1981	75.9	93.9

Source: Adapted from Walter Adams and James Brock, eds., *The Structure of American Industry*, 9th ed. (Englewood Cliffs, NJ: Prentice Hall, 1995).

speakeasies (which would put the alcohol back in), conveniently allow for the alcoholic beer to be stolen, or covertly transport it to speakeasies. The example of Cleveland is instructive. In 1919, a year before Prohibition, Cleveland had 1,200 legal bars. Three years after the onset of Prohibition, Cleveland was reported to have 3,000 illegal speakeasies, along with 10,000 stills. If an estimated 30,000 city residents sold liquor during Prohibition, another 100,000 were home brewers using malt syrup to concoct beer for friends.

The repeal of Prohibition in 1933 through the Twenty-first Amendment, which legalized beer with 3.2 percent alcohol, led several brewers to reopen. There were 765 brewers by 1930. Erstwhile leaders such as Anheuser-Busch and Pabst soon gained market share, and by the end of World War II, the number of breweries dropped to 468. Table 3.1 shows that from 1945 to 1980, the five largest breweries saw their market share grow from 19 percent to 75 percent as economies of scale in production, distribution, and advertising drove the sales of bottled beer.[14]

■ Industrial Beer as the Hot Cause and Cool Mobilization through Brewpubs

Remember that resource partitioning theory suggests that anti–mass production movements arise when a few large generalists dominate a market, leading to underserved market segments that specialists may exploit, even in the absence of scale economies.[15] Since generalist organizations offer homogeneous products with the broadest appeal, they can be attacked as inauthentic and low-quality producers, creating an opportunity for small organizations who can portray themselves as authentic, high-quality producers that embody local tastes, traditions, techniques, and voices. Generalist organizations that control large swathes of a market constitute psychologically salient targets for activists and potential entrepreneurs alike. In turn, psychologically salient targets of negative attention enable activists to dramatize a system's inherent contradictions and vulnerabilities and to articulate an insurgent identity in opposition to the dominant identity.[16]

However, a prerequisite for such action is discourse—discussion focuses public attention and creates cognitive space for arguments about possible solutions, which might include the development of new organizational forms.[17] Home brewing's discourse was supplied by the home-brewing movement that emerged in 1977–78. Although home brewing was illegal, experimenters such as Charles Papazian innovated beer-brewing techniques at home. As Papazian said in an interview, "I was by then doing home brewing as an avocation. Someone asked me to teach a class in Boulder. I taught 1,000 people in Colorado and was learning as I went—that grew, and in 1978, a friend and I put out a newsletter, *Zymurgy*, . . . it became a magazine for homebrewers. This activity grew into the concept of an association, and in 1978, I started the American Homebrewers Association."[18]

On February 1, 1979, home brewing was legalized by President Carter via an act of Congress introduced by Alan Cranston, a senator from California. It allowed individuals to brew a maximum of one hundred gallons per year for personal enjoyment. By 1984, the American Homebrewers Association (AHBA) had three thousand members, and its goal was to democratize the production of beer. It assailed the stranglehold of the Big Five beer producers (Busch, Pabst, Schlitz, Miller, and Coors).

The home-brewing movement educated consumers about traditional beers and artisanal techniques. It exacerbated the discontent among beer aficionados about the lack of choice and the dearth of fresh and tasteful beer sold at bars, restaurants, and other gathering places. Charles Papazian recounted that "'78, '79, '80, for me, was the homebrew focus. The microbrew concept was just an idea."[19]

The microbrew concept needed trained organization builders. A number of studies have shown that community-level organizational infrastructures to help activists are essential for a movement to develop. A denser organizational community is thus more fertile ground for founding new organizations because it provides human networks, loyalty, trust, organizing skills, and other assets necessary to found an organization.[20] The home-brewing movement provided such an infrastructure by fostering the growth of home-brewing clubs and created a "Beertown University" for aspiring home brewers. By 1998, there were more than 600 home-brewing clubs, as well as a full-fledged contest to evaluate the quality of home-brewed beer. By 1997, there were 1.5 million Americans who were home brewers according to the AHBA.

By 1981, microbreweries were "emerging. Home brewers were closest to it, and understood it. In 1983, the microbrewers split off and were institutionalized as a division of the AHBA. *Microbrewers were not home brewers any longer.*"[21] An early precursor was Fritz Maytag, who became an owner of Anchor Brewing in 1969 with the intention of providing some advice and leaving, but soon found himself drawn to brewing, and turned out traditional beers. By 1975 he was producing four distinctive beers. Arguably, the first microbrewery was set up by a sailor, Jack McAuliffe, who was accustomed to drinking Scottish ales. He became a dedicated home brewer after his return to the United States. In 1977 he established the New Albion Brewery in Sonoma with Suzy Stern and Jane Zimmerman to make ales.

Microbrewing received media attention when *Newsweek* ran a feature titled "The Battle of the Beers" in its September 4, 1978, issue, focusing on the battle between Busch and Miller, asserting that marketing and not brewing was the weapon of choice. The *Newsweek* article also gave attention to Anchor Steam and the smallest brewer in the land, New Albion.

Although New Albion had a short life, folding in 1983, it induced other home brewers to produce and market their beers. In 1982, Bert Grant opened the first brewpub in Yakima, Washington, the first place that not only brewed and sold beer on its premises but also sold food. Festivals like the Great American Beer Festival had begun educating consumers about the choices available in the market and provided a platform for aficionados to assess how their beer fared vis-à-vis other specialty beers. The Great American Beer Festival, established in 1982, drew about forty brewers and seven hundred beer enthusiasts.

These shots sparked a revolt against the beer establishment, and other enthusiasts started brewing in small quantities using traditional methods. The beer made by large brewers was disparaged as "industrial beer"—thin, tasteless, watery, and over-carbonated, a source of inebriation rather than taste. Michael Jackson, an eminent beer critic, recalled "beers that are bland or unpleasantly sticky-sweet, chicken-feedy, sort of too much corn, I think that's true of Corona and those types of beers, cheap standard beers in America and other countries. I'm tempted to ask the question, 'Why did they bother to make this? Why does this beer exist?'"[22]

One beer fan later lamented,

> Beer suffers from the sophomoric image promoted
> by the Big Three brewers. Their marketing promotes
> an image of beer as . . . *stuff*, something you have
> (but never drink, thanks to strange rules that do not

allow the portrayal of someone actually drinking beer), something that makes good times happen, something in a package, a bottle, a can, a glass. The infrequent ad that actually talks about the *beer* rather than the precious image is notable largely as an exception, and usually talks about the ingredients, the heritage, the process, but rarely the taste in more than extremely abstract terms. The "Carb War" is a classic example: they're talking about the beer, but in extracted numbers, worse than geeks with their IBU-strutting. And when Bud Light comes along and says "Choose on taste," you're left wondering: okay, what *does* it taste like?[23]

Despite these rhetorical attacks on Big Beer (i.e., the largest four producers), microbrewers and brewpubs pursued different market segments. The home brewers were not trying to take over the center of the market but to carve out niches at the edges. The beer critic Michael Jackson drew on several analogies to describe how Big Beer and microbrewing pursued different segments: "Small high-quality bakeries don't compete with Wonderbread. Gourmet food stores carrying real pasta don't threaten General Mills products. And that's how it works with microbreweries and brewpubs. . . . Microbrewery beers are consumed by people with adventurous tastes—not old line beer lovers except where there is a strong German influence."[24]

In their study of the microbrewing industry, Glenn Carroll and Anand Swaminathan have shown that as the concentration of market share by the largest four manufacturers rose, there was a greater opportunity for microbrewers and brewpubs to intensify the critique of Big Beer and pursue a different segment in the periphery. As concentration approaches 90 percent, the establishment of microbreweries and brewpubs is likely to go up 500 times compared to when the concentration is 12.6 percent. Concentration has the opposite effect on the failure rate of breweries: as concentration increases, the failure rate goes down.[25]

■ Organizational Foundations of the Microbrewing Movement

Charles Papazian recounted, "I thought it was the beginning of a movement, but I did not envision what that meant."[26] The early recruits to microbrewing were attorneys, financiers, businesspeople, teachers, oceanographers, some brewery workers, and retail shop owners. Carol Stoudt, the only woman microbrewery owner in the early years, who started her career as a teacher, described her journey to ownership in 1988: "Three years ago I would have told anyone they were crazy if they said I was going to do this. I never even drank beer. At fraternity parties I used to slip into the ladies' room and pour my beer down the toilet. . . . One night I stopped at a restaurant and met the owner, who was the man who would be my husband. He dated and romanced me to Germany, and there I learned that beer could be good. And I got caught up in the romance of the small brewer. Five years ago in the Northwest, we toured twenty small breweries. We saw that beers could be unique to an area. All those influences inspired us to make a brewery."[27]

The passion to make tasteful beer with traditional artisanal techniques induced early microbrewers and brewpub owners to enter the industry. Their spirit was exemplified by Bob Connors of the Independence Brewing Company, whose billboard read "Independence—enjoy it while it lasts." As Fritz Maytag put it in an interview, "The more breweries there are, the more it will help all of us. We are like bacteria in a bottle. Alone we mean nothing, but if there are a lot of us, we can make a difference."[28] The numbers of new microbreweries and brewpubs increased in tandem: microbrews and brewpubs legitimized each other and enhanced each other's cultural acceptance.[29]

In a talk to the Craft Brewers Conference in 2004, Gary Fish, the president of Deschutes Brewery of Bend, Oregon, said, "There is an old Chinese proverb that says, 'Enough shovels of earth, a mountain, enough pails of water, a river.' We are that mountain and that river." By 1994, close to 500 establishments were part of the $400 million craft beer movement in the United States, and microbrewers crafted more than two million barrels of beer—which produced revenues much less than the total sales of Michelob Light. As a craft movement, then, the microbreweries and brewpubs were by definition less about scale and more an expression of a new identity, one premised on small-scale, authentic, and traditional methods of production, and fresh beer with myriad tastes. As aficionados armed with small kettles, fresh ingredients, and unique recipes began to produce a stunning variety of beers, other beer lovers sought to solidify the identity of craft brewing by establishing an infrastructure to support the craft-brewing movement.

■ Stealth Micros and the Identity of Microbrewers

Microbrewers potentially jeopardized the business model of Big Beer, which relied on economies of scale in mass production, marketing, and distribution of beer. Big producers initially responded by creating semi-autonomous divisions that introduced beers designed to emulate microbrews. Coors established the Unibev division that launched Killian's Red and later Blue Moon; Miller Beer formed the Specialty Craft Brewing Unit that introduced Plank Road Brews; and Anheuser-Busch's Specialty Brewing Unit pushed the Pacific Ridge line of beers. These were so-called stealth micros because in their efforts to emulate micros they did not rely on the parent's brand and thereby concealed their Big Beer origins to consumers. The reason, as one Miller Brewing executive said, is that consumers "think that all [products brewed by a particular brewery] taste the same, and their mind is closed."[30] These attempts to "fake" microbrews were quickly exposed as inauthentic through the network of beer clubs, brewing guilds, and fans with Web sites.

Big Beer producers also began to take equity positions in microbrewers but did not seek to undermine the identity of microbrewers and brewpubs and instead left them as standalone operations. If Busch took an ownership position in Red Hook and formed an alliance with Widmer Brothers, Miller bought controlling equity in Celis. But even these alliances, as Sam Calagione, the owner of the Dogfish Head Brewery, said in his keynote address to at the craftbrewers conference in Seattle in 2006, threaten the unique *terroir*—the sense of place or the special characteristics of geography that bestow individuality.

The *terroir* of beer producers is at the heart of their claims to a distinctive and authentic identity. Small size (a maximum of 15,000 barrels of production), on-site brewing, and the use of artisanal techniques define an authentic microbrewer or brewpub, and any attempt to violate these characteristics is met with criticism and invites sanctions. A telling instance of this was the attempt of "contract brewers," those who do not own their brewing facilities and instead contract out production to others, to pass as craft brewers. Contract brewers are another manifestation of "stealth micros" because they conceal their lack of ownership but can expand their operations quickly. Some of them, such as Boston Beer Company (the maker of Sam Adams) and Pete's Brewing Company (producers of Pete's Wicked Ale), are quite visible. Contract brewers grew quickly, and by 1997, 114 of them were in operation.[31]

Investment bankers extolled contract brewing as a business model. One such report pointed out that the cumulative annual growth rate of contract brewers from 1985 until 1994 was 38 percent in comparison to 23 percent for microbrewers and 30 percent for brewpubs. They argued that contract brewers were likely to grow at 40 percent annually because they had three potent advantages over microbrewers and brewpubs: they needed less capital than microbrews or brewpubs because they could contract out, they could invest more in marketing and sales, and they could grow more quickly.[32]

Microbrewers and brewpub owners assailed contract brewing. Fritz Maytag, the éminence grise of microbrewing, said, "We're sticking to our original goals. I want to make all our beer right here in this building. Hands on. . . . And then there are the folks . . . the farming-out companies, who contract with different breweries. Pete's Wicked does 600,000 to 800,000 barrels a year, and Sam Adams more than a million. These pseudo micros are a response to the demand that we helped create back in the late '70s and early '80s. I hate to be pejorative, but a contract brewer is a marketing company—'We'll market it if you brew it.'"[33] In a similar vein, Michael Jackson, the beer critic, averred,

> I think one is always going to feel slightly uncomfortable about contract brewing. It's something that confuses the issue too, like what is a microbrewed beer and what isn't a microbrewed beer. I wonder about the staying power of some of the big contract brewers. I think it's true that you can, in certain circumstances, produce a very good beer by contract brewing. But some of the big contract brewers are run by marketing. I wonder if you slack off the advertising at all, does the thing just collapse? . . . The small brewing industry sliding towards the marketing men again. I've often joked that there should be a cull of marketing men once a year, and that they should just sort of take one in 10 and shoot them. There are some very good marketing people, but for every good marketing person, there are about 10 [expletive deleted]. That's a very bad influence on the industry.[34]

Big Beer producers who were threatened by the growth of contract brewers also launched a campaign calling for truth-in-advertising and targeted Boston Beer. NBC's *Dateline* program also ran an exposé of contract brewing and charged them with misleading consumers.

Contract brewers like Jim Koch of Boston Beer vehemently disagreed. "We're all in the same minor league," he said. "We and Anchor—we're a millionth of Budweiser. That's the big guy. Yes, we may be bigger than Anchor, but that doesn't matter. It's in the brewing. Contract brewing versus a vat in the back room just doesn't matter, and Fritz knows that. Who owns the kettle and where the kettle is—it's a meaningless thing."[35] Koch even argued that closeness to the customer meant freshness.

Did contract brewers grow as the investment banking report predicted? Or was their growth constrained because of their impaired claims to authenticity? Carroll and Swaminathan found that exposure to brewpubs rather than microbrews undermined contract brewers. Brewpubs were a vivid representation of small size, local diversity, and artisanal production and a stronger manifestation of craft brewing than microbrews. The more the number of brewpubs increased, the more the number of contract brewers decreased and the sooner they went out of business.[36]

■ Implications

Thus, the renaissance of microbrewing was fueled by a social movement populated by beer lovers and enthusiasts—evange-ale-ists who rebelled against the dominance of the market by Big Beer. On the face of it, a high concentration of market shares is an omen of the lack of opportunity. Microbrewers succeeded because the concentration of market shares provided them with an opportunity that they exploited through skillful framing and rhetorical attacks on Big Beer. More important, they rapidly mobilized themselves by setting up small, artisanal organizations and constructed an identity that inoculated themselves against the threat of entry by Big Beer or contract brewers. Neither could surmount the obstacle of authenticity despite their efforts.

The saga of microbrewing's success stands in remarkable contrast to the failure of the pirate radio movement to construct an opportunity and effectively mobilize.[37] Pirate radio—unlicensed, illegitimate broadcasts, often run by individuals using mobile transmitters and irregular program schedules so as to avoid detection and enforcement—was an outlet of self-expression for those who felt that traditional radio did not feature diverse local voices, minorities, or controversial points of view. Stephen Dunipher, a key figure during the pirate era and founder of the pirate station Free Radio Berkeley, a fifty-watt station that broadcast round the clock (originally from his own apartment), exemplified the ideals of the pirate radio movement. He sought to correct what he perceived as a pro-government bias in media reporting on the first Gulf War and hoped to get the public involved in broadcasting on unlicensed microradio stations, thus creating an "ungovernable situation" for the Federal Communications Commission (FCC), ultimately forcing the FCC to legalize low-power, non-commercial broadcasting. The key to this strategy was open civil disobedience aimed at drawing the FCC into a public legal battle where it would be forced to justify its licensing policies. The pirate rhetoric framed the FCC as the enemy and their solution was civil disobedience.

While the pirates may have had a hot cause—the FCC—they did not have cool mobilization. The pirates' campaign to create chaos on the airwaves failed to produce numbers sufficient to force the FCC's hand. The FCC responded primarily by tracking pirate transmissions, shutting down the stations, confiscating the equipment, and jailing operators. The National Association of Broadcasters (NAB), the broadcast industry's lobbying group, increased pressure on the FCC to shut down pirate operations as they proliferated. Commercial radio broadcasters would hire their own personnel to check for signal interference and issue complaints to the FCC. The master strategy the pirates employed—civil disobedience and resistance—simply did not resonate with the general public in the mid-1990s. Neither, apparently, did the extremely liberal and often radical viewpoints voiced by most pirates; the movement's self-definition as an identity in sharp contrast to dominant popular culture alienated and excluded many potential supporters. Moreover, the loosely organized movement promoting the pirate frame did not appeal to other organizations or movements that might have helped promote its agenda. Therefore, despite the consistency of its message and the dedication of its members, the pirate frame was ultimately unsuccessful in achieving its goal of legalizing low-power radio.

Only later, when a new generation of rebels framed the ownership of radio stations by corporate chains and the domination of local radio markets by chains as the hot cause of soulless diversity, did they succeed. Chain ownership was a hot cause that galvanized public interest, and the cool mobilization was accomplished via lots of small-scale stations that added to the stock of cultural diversity. The Telecommunications Act of 1996 increased the limit on ownership of radio stations in a single market from two to eight stations and eliminated the limit on nationwide ownership. In the two years following the passage of the act, approximately 50 percent of the radio stations in the United States changed hands, most going from independent to corporate ownership. In 2001, Clear Channel Communications alone owned 1,238 stations, or 11 percent of all stations, whereas Viacom/Infinity owned 184 stations, and Citadel Communications owned 206 stations. Such consolidation allowed radio chains to replace local news programming and personalities with syndicated programming and replicate formats nationwide. One indicator of growing homogenization was that the number of songs entering the weekly top 10 declined from 114 in 1995 to 59 in 2000.[38]

Micro-radio activists seized on chains as the enemy; former pirates such as Dunifer or Pete Tridish, media reform advocates such as the Media Access Project, and Christian evangelists banded together to replace the homogeneity of chains with local voices on the air through low-power FM radio service. The ensuing Micro-radio Empowerment Coalition forged connections with "the Green Party, the United States Catholic Conference, the Library Association of America, the ACLU, the Council of Calvin Christian Reformed Church, Native American tribes and the United Church of Christ; celebrities like the Indigo Girls, Bonnie Raitt, and Kurt Vonnegut; and the cities of Detroit, Seattle, Ann Arbor, Mich., and Santa Monica, Berkeley and Richmond, Calif., among others."[39] Micro-radio activists found

William Kennard, the FCC chairman, to be a valuable ally, and they were able to overcome the objections of the National Association of Broadcasters and even NPR to win the right to broadcast for religious, community, or educational purposes, without advertisements. Their operations were limited to an effective radiated power (ERP) of 100 watts (0.1 kilowatts) or less and maximum facilities of 100 watts ERP at 30 meters (100 feet) antenna height above average terrain (HAAT), giving them a broadcast radius of approximately 3.5 miles.

Predictably, the greatest number of applications to start low-power FM radio stations were received by the FCC for markets where chain domination was the highest, and in turn, it was the diversity of applicants that played a decisive role in the selection of applicants by the FCC.[40] More important, the diversity of low-powered FM radio stations significantly increased LPFM listening as measured by both diary mentions and quarter-hours; organizational diversity enables social movements to reach out to different audiences, when the outputs are cultural.[41]

But did the low-power FM radio movement reduce the concentration of chains? The sheer number or density of low-powered FM radio stations had no effect—unsurprisingly—on the concentration of market shares by chain-owned radio stations. The idea of resource partitioning suggests that concentration in the center of the market frees up peripheral resources; as a result, there is little overlap between generalists and specialists. This is also ironic because the salient enemy motivating the low-powered FM radio movement was the concentration of market shares in local markets in the hands of chain-owned radio stations. Activists condemned chains, and mobilized organization building, but the new organizations catered to completely different audiences. Surprisingly, initial increases in LPFM founder diversity increased chain concentration, but subsequent increases in founder diversity lowered it. Thus, low-powered FM radio stations initially hurt non-chain-owned commercial stations, and then were able to make a dent on chains. So the diversity of protest organizations, rather than the density, is critical for social movements seeking to affect popular culture through organizational proliferation.[42]

Social movements arise in concentrated industries when there is a *hot cause* and succeed when there is a *cool mobilization*; microbrewing succeeded because industrial producers were made the enemy, and artisanal production was the mechanism of mobilization, but the pirate radio movement failed because the FCC was made into the enemy initially, and civil disobedience was proffered as the basis of mobilization. By contrast, the low-powered FM radio movement thrived because chain ownership was the *hot cause,* and *cool mobilization* took the form of low-cost "guerilla" radio stations that catered to the community.

The beer and radio examples pertain to a mature market and nicely counterpoint the case of the automobile industry. A natural extension is to consider whether and how collective action shapes markets featuring "high culture" products—painting, opera, classical music, or gastronomy. These markets encompass the creative arts, and they have been assailed as suffering from a "cost disease," a concept first proposed by the economists William Baumol and William

Bowen.[43] The amount of time it takes four musicians to play a Beethoven string quartet has remained constant since the 1800s—thus arts productivity cannot really keep pace with the rest of the economy. If there is such a cost disease, how does radical technological change that leads to new products and processes occur in the creative arts? In chapter 4, I turn to this question by analyzing how a new style of cuisine emerged in French gastronomy as a result of the nouvelle cuisine movement, which led to new products and processes.

The French Revolution
Collective Action and the Nouvelle Cuisine Innovation

December 16, 1897, was a red-letter day in the systematization of classical French cuisine. On that day, Auguste Escoffier composed the first menu at the Ritz Hotel in London and started the practice of serving each dish in the order printed on the menu. Before Escoffier's innovation, each course had consisted of a number of related dishes that were served en masse on the table, and patrons were invited to choose among them. Escoffier's first menu (see table 4.1) is striking because it reflected the building blocks of classical cuisine: heavy soups such as beef consommé thickened with arrow-root and turtle fat, elaborate sauces (for instance, turbot in a sauce of Volnay wine), meat dishes with elaborate garnishes such as chicken stuffed with rice and decked with truffles, game birds such as spit-roasted snipe, thick desserts like the Sicilian bombe (a lemon ice cream made with thirty-two egg yolks), and place-names for dishes such as salads from the Perigord.

Classical cuisine as codified by Escoffier endured for more than three-quarters of a century. Ironically, Ho-Chi-Minh, who started a revolution in North Vietnam, served Es-coffier as a cook's helper and reportedly became a pastry chef under him. Some historical accounts suggest that Escoffier invited Ho-Chi-Minh to set aside his revolutionary ideas and learn the art of cooking but that Ho-Chi-Minh demurred.

Table 4.1
Escoffier's First Menu: December 16, 1897

Hors d'oeuvre

Caviar and blinis

Consomme of beef, chicken, and turtle, thickened with arrowroot,
garnished with diced turtle and Madeira wine

Chicken consommé, garnished with shoots

Young turbot with a sauce of Volnay wine, garnished with lettuce

Sole filleted and cooked in butter, dressed in timbale with a garnish
of small potatoes, slices of truffles rolled in meat glaze

Poularde fillets with truffles

Beans from the Marais

Venison with minced mushrooms and shallots

Chestnut souffle

Crayfish with pepper sauce, juniper berries, Marsala

Sorbet rose

Spit-roasted snipes

Celeriac salad from Perigord

Argentuil asparagus

Foie gras poached in Rhone wine

Sicilian bombe

Fruity millefeuille

Thus, while one of Escoffier's employees went on to lead a revolution elsewhere, classical cuisine remained undisturbed for several decades.

It was only in 1972 that a band of young, rebellious French chefs—Paul Bocuse, Alain Chapel, Michel Guérard,

George Blanc, and the Troisgros brothers—aided by two culinary journalists, Henri Gault and Christian Millau, led a revolution that subverted the tenets of classical cuisine. Had one visited Maison Troisgros in the early 1970s, the menu would have featured very different cooking techniques than Escoffier's, with methods that emphasized freshness, natural flavors, and exotic spices. Instead of the foie gras soaked in Rhone wine as in Escoffier's Ritz, one might have encountered foie gras with Chinese cabbage and grilled groundnuts. Similarly, Escoffier's crayfish in muscovite sauce might have yielded to a fricassee of lobster, the fish in heavy sauces would have been replaced by line-caught fish served grilled, and instead of the venison drenched in sauce, one would encounter grilled calf sweetbreads. The heavy millefeuille dessert would have been replaced by a granita of mocha. This was the nouvelle cuisine revolution.

How did classical cuisine succumb? The method of its demise and the rise of nouvelle cuisine provide an interesting glimpse into the social sources of radical technological change in creative industries such as the arts, music, food, and drama.

As alluded to in chapter 3, creative industries suffer from a "cost disease" and lag in productivity behind the general economy. In such industries, the conditions of production inhibit radical technological change because the "work of the performer is an end in itself."[1] String quartets are not peddling something beyond a given performance; they are not trying to give the consumer more Beethoven for the buck. If this is the case, how does disruptive technological change lead to new products and new processes in the creative arts? More specifically, creative industries, as the sociologist Howard Becker suggests, feature artworlds—networks of cooperative production among artists, support personnel, critics, and the final consumer—which are governed by conventions that specify the materials to be used, and the techniques that are employed require cooperation among the various actors.[2] Conventions constrain innovation; support personnel and gatekeepers have incentives to preserve the status quo. How are conventions breached?

In this chapter I draw on my research on haute cuisine restaurants in France during the period 1970–97 to demonstrate how collective action spurred the ascent of nouvelle cuisine as a style, and rebels articulated a *hot cause*— freedom from Escoffier—and relied on *cool mobilization* through fresh, exotic ingredients and improvisation by chefs. The nouvelle cuisine movement sought to transform the identity of the chef from a technician following the instructions of Escoffier into an inventor. Once the heat that divided nouvelle cuisine from classical cuisine dissipated, it became cool for chefs to borrow and blend ingredients and techniques from both styles.[3] French gastronomy is a creative industry and its high-brow status contrasts nicely with the worlds of beer and radio that we explored in chapter 3. Moreover, French gastronomy is interesting because restaurants pursue profits by selling short-lived experiences.

■ The Codification of Classical Cuisine as a Style

The French Revolution of 1789 undermined the logic of cuisine in the ancien régime, wherein meals were public spectacles organized according to hierarchy and the chef was virtually owned by patrons or nobles. But after the French Revolution, chefs who once worked in the houses of private patrons offered their services to the public by establishing restaurants in Paris and its environs. Haute cuisine shifted from private homes into public restaurants, the spectacle of the banquet was replaced by a more intimate encounter, the hierarchy of the banquet of the ancien régime was supplanted by a more egalitarian order, and the extravagance of banquets gave way to economy.[4]

An informal and decentralized effort to systematize the principles of this cuisine was led by chefs and gastronomic journalists. Among these writers, the most influential was Antonin Carème (1784–1833), a chef who worked in the houses of great patrons such as Talleyrand. He pioneered the effort to systematize the principles of the modern cuisine that emerged after the French Revolution. Carème disparaged the old cuisine of the ancien régime because it did not mesh with the zeitgeist of post-revolutionary France, and in his *Philosophical History of Cuisine* (1833) he created a vision of *grande cuisine* as both an art and a science. He simplified meals so that there were four courses at dinner instead of eight, gave more space to those sitting at the table, and sought to redefine humble dishes such as pot-au-feu as the essence of a French cuisine. He and his disciples produced sauces that were works of art; sauces such as bourguignonne, salmis, sauce suprème, or sauce hollandaise camouflaged the meat, game, or fish being served rather than enhancing their flavor. Stressing delicacy, order, and economy, Carème brought symmetry to the service of meals and introduced a new awareness of freshness and sanitation into the French kitchen. Carème's ideas quickly diffused throughout the kitchens of Parisian restaurants, as well as the rest of France, and reshaped the culinary culture of the times.[5]

Carème's ideas were strengthened by a new breed of chefs, which included Georges Auguste Escoffier (1847–1935) and his circle of collaborators—including his friend Prosper Montagné (1865–1948), author of the *Larousse Gastronomique* (1938), who worked in the kitchens of fashionable hotels that had been established in the major cities of Europe, notably by César Ritz, toward the end of the nineteenth century. If Carème's books constituted the Old Testament, Escoffier's *Guide Culinaire*, first published in 1903, was the New Testament that formed the body of what came to be known as classical cuisine, and it remains a central text in the training of professional cooks. Escoffier wrote down dishes in the order of presentation (*service à la Russe*), and developed the first à la carte menu. He simplified the art of cooking by getting rid of ostentatious food displays and elaborate garnishes, and reduced the number of courses served. He emphasized the use of seasonal foods and urged that sauces be used to reveal the flavors of game, meat, and fish rather than to conceal them. Escoffier simplified professional kitchen organization, integrating it into a single unit from its previously individualized sections that operated autonomously and led to waste and duplication of labor. It was during the Escoffier era that French haute cuisine achieved the undisputed international hegemony that it had begun to acquire since the Restoration. In the preface to the 1907 edition of *Guide Culinaire,* Escoffier summarized classical cuisine as follows: "In a word, cookery whilst continuing to be an art will become scientific and will have to submit its formulas which very often are still too empirical, to a method and precision which leaves nothing to chance."

He conceived of classical cuisine as codified grammar of culinary practice: a product can be *cooked* in different ways, *served* with different sauces, and *accompanied* by different fillings. Escoffier's guide was issued in several editions and remained the dominant orthodoxy until it was undermined by the nouvelle cuisine movement. The French culinary writer Claude Fischler identified five dimensions to understanding the cultural logic and role of identity of classical cuisine: culinary rhetoric, rules of cooking, archetypal ingredients used, the role of the chef, and the organization of the menu.[6] Table 4.2 displays these dimensions.[7]

The culinary rhetoric of classical cuisine reveals the emphasis on conservatism and preservation. Often, dishes were named after the places, noblemen, or mythological characters associated with them. Moreover, cooking consisted of the application of two principles: conformation to the rules formulated by Carème and Escoffier, and sublimation of the ingredients such that the raw material was visually transformed. The archetypal ingredients used were high game, shellfish, cream, poultry, and river fish. The menu was organized so that it consisted of a long list and required substantial inventories in the restaurant. The chef was an employee of the restaurant-owner and remained in the background.

Table 4.2
The Classical Cuisine Code

Culinary Rhetoric	Names of dishes refer to rhetoric, memory, and legitimacy
Rules of Cooking	*Conformation,* or staying in conformity with Escoffier's principles: gratins and quenelles, terrines, pâtés, confits, jambons, jambonneaux, saucissons, boudins, andouillettes
	Sublimation, or sublimating the ingredients: brioches, croûtes, vessies, farces, émincés, chaussons, croustades, vol au vent, sauces, flambages (flambé), bisques, délices, dodines, timbales, Chateaubriand
Archetypal Ingredients	High game, shellfish, cream, poultry, river fish
Role of the Chef	The restaurateur, rarely the owner, and never the cook, has the power in the rooms of luxury hotels and palaces. The classical service is organized through the saucepan. The waiters cut and serve the dishes, blaze ("flambé") preparations. The rituals are outside the plate.
Organization of the Menu	Extremely long menu, almost all the classical dishes are registered. Need for large inventories, therefore less freshness. Consuming is a long ceremony. Related art is *Architecture* (three dimensions). Relief and contours are important. One sense is critical: vision.

The rituals of dining prominently featured the waiter, who cut and served dishes, flambéed the preparations, and organized the service through the saucepan. Fischler summarized it as follows: "The art of the cook consisted in accommodating, in transforming, in metamorphosing the raw material, to put it from Nature to Culture. . . . The maître queux was a kind of grand 'sophisticator,' in the etymologic sense of 'falsificator.'"[8]

This logic and role identity of chefs became institutionalized through a network of training schools such as Le Cordon Bleu and professional societies such as the Association des Maîtres Queux. Although it was started in 1896 to provide training to housewives, Le Cordon Bleu began offering courses in haute cuisine classique from 1900 that were first overseen by Charles Driessens, then by Mademoiselle Distel from 1904 until 1930, and later by Henri-Paul Pellaprat for several decades. In 1950, forty chefs trained in haute cuisine classique established the Association des Maîtres Queux to certify master chefs who were exponents of haute cuisine and to ensure the highest standards of professional excellence. Classical cuisine reigned supreme for three decades after Escoffier's death in 1935 because of such training schools and societies. Such was the ascendancy of classical cuisine that the magazine *Le Cordon Bleu* had twenty-five thousand subscribers in 1930 and became a drawing card in its own right.

■ Autonomy as the Hot Cause and Improvisation as Cool Mobilization

Nouvelle cuisine arose because the events of May 1968 exposed contradictions between two values: conformity to Escoffier and the autonomy of the chef. Just as the French Revolution was the master movement that led to the death knell of ancien régime cuisine and the construction of classical cuisine by Carème and other gastronomic writers, the events of May 1968 triggered the decline of classical cuisine and the growth of the nouvelle cuisine movement. Fischler writes,

> The Grande Cuisine, at the end of the 1960s, experiences a kind of revolution and revelation. Beyond this sudden vogue, there is a larger wave, one of wide-ranging social and economical movements that had been transforming the French society, and wavelets, those that the larger wave indirectly induced in the Cuisine and catering industries. The Grande Gastronomy crystallizes and precipitates latent trends in the society. . . . When studying the nature and content of the Nouvelle Cuisine, one could perceive a large part of further evolutions in the attitudes and behaviors in France.[9]

The larger wave was the protests of May 1968, which hastened the wavelet of nouvelle cuisine. On May 6, 1968, students at the Sorbonne who were protesting against the punishment meted out to eight students at Nanterre for their opposition to the Vietnam War were attacked by police on the Boulevard St. Germain. Scores of students were arrested, and many students and policemen were injured. Soon students mobilized with marches, decried examinations as a rite of initiation into capitalism, called for the triumph of the "general will over the General" (De Gaulle), and sought to create a society that valued personal autonomy and eliminated distinctions between those who gave orders and those who took them. France was on the verge of a revolution with twelve million workers on strike, 122 factories occupied by workers, and students battling against an authoritarian system. The anti-authoritarian wave of May 1968 amplified the effect of undercurrents already visible in the literary, theater, film, and culinary worlds through the *le nouveau roman, la nouvelle critique, le nouveau théâtre,* and *la nouvelle vague* anti-schools. All of these anti-schools shared similar conceptual principles and challenged convention, hierarchy, and rules.

The nouvelle cuisine movement was an echo of these anti-schools; its first stirrings appeared in 1965 and were visible in 1972. Nouvelle cuisine was shaped and promoted by activists in the center of the French culinary world, chefs who had received the highest honors from the French state and had garnered plaudits from the *Guide Michelin.* Nouvelle cuisine was a bid to enhance the professional autonomy of chefs. Under classical cuisine chefs possessed the freedom to establish their own restaurants in classical cuisine and design their menus, and celebrity chefs with three Michelin stars could also control financial promoters. However, no matter how well trained chefs were, they lacked technical autonomy because their role was to translate the intentions or prescriptions of Escoffier into products. Under classical cuisine, chefs lacked the freedom to create and invent dishes, and the nouvelle cuisine movement sought to make chefs into inventors rather than mere technicians.

Paul Bocuse and other activists were able to denounce the lack of autonomy for chefs in classical cuisine because their criticisms resonated with the sentiments against hierarchy that were gaining ground after the events of May 1968 and were also in tune with the avant-garde movements in the literary and artistic worlds. Bocuse and other co-evangelists exploited the ideas of simplicity and economy in classical cuisine to fashion a new logic and a new identity for chefs. Just as students in Nantes and film directors such as Godard challenged old rules such as exams or a stylized sequence of shots, Bocuse and his allies questioned culinary conventions and exhorted chefs to engage in culinary invention. In an echo of the students' protests against ostentation and fakery and film-makers' struggle for realism, the Troisgros brothers and Alain Chapel wanted simplicity and economy of presentation. If literary critics like Barthes and Derrida sought to portray the reader as a creator of meaning, Bocuse and Chapel wanted chefs to have a role in creating and inventing dishes rather than simply understanding the intentions of Escoffier. Table 4.3 displays the nouvelle cuisine code.[10]

Nouvelle cuisine relied on the rules of transgression and acclimatization. Transgression consisted of using old cooking techniques with new ingredients or with old ingredients in illegitimate ways, mixing meat and fish, creating salads that mixed vegetables and foie gras, and serving pot-au-feu with fish. Acclimatization meant importing exotic foreign cuisine traditions, notably seasoning and spices. Two influences can be identified: the influence from Japanese cuisine during the late 1970s, when most of the evangelists traveled to Japan, and the growing influence of former colonies and immigrants.[11] The ingredients of nouvelle cuisine included fruits, vegetables, potatoes, aromatic herbs, exotic ingredi-

Table 4.3
Nouvelle Cuisine Code

Culinary Rhetoric	Appellations refer to poetry, imagination, and evocation: small (petit), diminutives, émincés, allégés; symphonies, trilogies, menus, assiettes
Rules of Cooking	*Transgression*: using old cooking techniques with new ingredients or with old ingredients: mixing meat and fish; a salad mixing vegetables and foie gras; pot-au-feu with fish
	Acclimatization: importing "exotic" foreign cuisine traditions, notably seasoning and spices, including fresh pasta, ravioli, cannelloni, cheesecake, cappuccino, crumble, carpaccio, pudding, presskopf, risotto, tajine
Archetypal Ingredients	Fruits, vegetables, potatoes, aromatic herbs, exotic ingredients, sea fish
Role of the Chef	The chef is at the center of operations. With "service à la japonaise" (service through the plate and service under a *cloche*), waiters' role minimized.
Organization of the Menu	Very narrow menu, even no menu: chefs propose "Cuisine du Marché," "Cuisine selon saison." No inventories to increase freshness. Consuming is a shorter ceremony.
	Related art is *Painting* (two dimensions): service through the plate leads cooks to add products only for aesthetic reasons. Colors, contrasts, decoration, and the five senses are important.

ents, and sea fish. The role of the chef was reframed to that of an innovator, creator, and owner, and the role of the waiter was minimized. *Service à la japonaise* or service through the plate (first offered by Troisgros in the late 1960s) and service under a *cloche* (first presented by Guérard in the early 1970s) minimized the role of the waiter. The nouvelle cuisine menu was far shorter than the classical cuisine menu and large inventories became superfluous since chefs emphasized freshness. Service through the plate and service under a cloche led cooks to add products only for aesthetic reasons, emphasizing colors, contrasts, and decoration but in a shorter ceremony. The object of nouvelle cuisine was "no more the metamorphosis of the food product, but the revelation of its essential truth."[12]

Interviews with chefs suggested that dissatisfaction with their own knowledge and the desire for autonomy were triggers of identity change for key activists. Michel Guérard, a winner of three Michelin stars and the Meilleurs Ouvriers de France in cooking and pastry, was a nouvelle cuisine activist who rejected classical cuisine. Guérard, speaking of himself and Jean Delaveyne, who also started as a pastry chef, said, "Classical cuisine itself had been lifeless, inert, apathetic for a while. . . . The desire emerged in us to do something else, to singularize ourselves, to be recalcitrant and reject the traditional authority and whatever existed before."[13]

The conversion of Gilles Etéocle, chef of La Poularde, located in Montrond-les-Bains, a large village in a sparsely populated, agriculture-based area in central France, shows how chefs had to respond to old customers while embracing nouvelle cuisine and manage the transition. La Poularde, awarded two stars since 1967, is the oldest two-star French restaurant, and Johannes Randoing, a cook since 1934, was succeeded by his son-in-law, Gilles Etéocle, in 1988. Etéocle declared in an interview with the author,

> We are a family business. My father-in law cooked a very rich cuisine. We used up to 200 liters of cream a week, down to 15 liters a week now. The sauce drove all the cuisine. The sauce was the quintessence. . . . There is an old cook's saying: "If you are not capable of some sorcery, it is not worth getting involved in cuisine." The sauce chef was the alchemist. At that time, the customers came for that cuisine. When I took over in the mid 80s . . . I started to innovate and proposed a more personal cuisine. However, it was very complicated to have two ethics living under the same roof. When loyal old customers come along and tell you: "it is no more what it used to [be], there is no more Creole rice to sponge up the sauce. . . ." It has taken more than fifteen years for me to affirm my spirit in my cuisine. . . . Now, I have done it, I am in coherence with my cuisine. You know, it is an art; I have been on the edge for years to keep this second star.

■ Was Nouvelle Cuisine a Fad?

As a motor of collective action, social movements differ from fads and fashions in that they are organized efforts to reorganize a social field and result in enduring social change. To address whether nouvelle cuisine was a short-lived fad, information on the temporal pattern of abandonment of classical cuisine and adoption of nouvelle cuisine is required. One way to study whether chefs subscribe to classical or nouvelle cuisine is to understand their signature dishes, which chefs identify as emblematic of their identity. They are sources of pride for the chef. Each year, the Michelin guide lists three signature dishes of any chef in a given restaurant who received a star. These are dishes submitted by the chef to the Michelin guide, and the only requirement is that they ought to be a regular feature of the menu and easily available to consumers. Consumers who see the guide and the signature dishes of a restaurant can easily decide whether to patronize the restaurant.[14]

In 1970, when our window of observation begins with the onset of the nouvelle cuisine movement, 47.69 percent of chefs had all three signature dishes in classical cuisine; only 2.26 percent had all three signature dishes in nouvelle cuisine. By 1997, only 6.32 percent of chefs were all classical, and 30.83 percent were all nouvelle cuisine. In 1970, 225 chefs (35.77 percent) had one nouvelle cuisine dish (and, by implication, two classical cuisine dishes). Chefs in 1970 considered one nouvelle cuisine dish a trial and did not take risks; in many cases, they copied Troisgros's l'escalope de saumon à l'oseille. Thus, at the outset of the movement, there was interest in nouvelle cuisine. If dominantly classical cuisine chefs are defined as those with no or one nouvelle cuisine dish, they accounted for 83.46 percent of chefs in 1970, but by 1997 this number had declined to only 29.84 percent, and 70.16 percent of chefs were dominantly nouvelle cuisine, having two or more signature dishes in the nouvelle realm. Nouvelle cuisine steadily gained adherents over time, and classical cuisine eroded over time, which is consistent with the growth of a social movement rather than a fad.

Did chefs merely flirt with nouvelle cuisine only to abandon it later? The majority of those who had one or more nouvelle cuisine dishes did not abandon them wholesale.[15] In 1975, 84.8 percent of nouvelle cuisine adoptees did not abandon even one nouvelle cuisine dish for classical cuisine, and this number remained as high as 74.3 percent in 1997. Chefs abandoning one nouvelle dish for a classical dish rose from 14.9 percent in 1975 to 25.6 percent in 1997, thereby indicating some degree of hybridization. But none of the chefs with three nouvelle cuisine dishes abandoned them for classical cuisine, and less than 1 percent of chefs with two nouvelle cuisine dishes abandoned them for classical cuisine in 1975 and 1987. The average time since adoption of a nouvelle cuisine dish ranged from 0 to 144 months, with a mean of 28.8 months, indicating that people did not adopt nouvelle cuisine and abandon it shortly thereafter.

■ How Did Collective Action Succeed in Establishing Nouvelle Cuisine?

In the nouvelle cuisine movement, culinary rebels were exhorting chefs to change not just their menus but their identity: to be innovators and not slaves to Escoffier. More than delivering exhortations, they were offering a new theory of cuisine. Theories can originate from many places, ranging from academic researchers to journalists, and can be communicated to the public via various types of media.[16] Journalists are interesting sources of theories because they have a predisposition to cover newsworthy disruptions and celebrate the differences between the old logic and identity and the insurgent logic and identity. Media coverage of innovations is seldom neutral and often laudatory, and a study of media coverage of quality circles reported that 85 percent of references were laudatory.[17]

In the case of nouvelle cuisine, culinary journalists sympathetic to nouvelle cuisine played an important role in creating a shared symbolic environment for chefs and the public to appreciate the new logic and identity. A monthly periodical was created in 1972 by Henri Gault and Christian Millau, two culinary journalists, to advance nouvelle cuisine, and Gault and Millau went on to encapsulate the "Ten Commandments of Nouvelle Cuisine" in *Vive la Nouvelle Cuisine Française*. These ten commandments reflect four values, which also characterized the protests of May 1968: truth, lightness, simplicity, and imagination. Culinary journalists writing in magazines such as *Le Cuisinier Français* (published since 1934) and newer culinary journals such as *La Revue Thuries* (published since 1988) propagated nouvelle cuisine by popularizing its virtues, advancing rationales for the adoption of nouvelle cuisine, and chronicling success stories of conversion and innovation. Favorable media coverage of nouvelle cuisine by culinary journalists undermined the logic of classical cuisine, created a discrepancy between members' desire for a positive social identity and their current affiliation, and induced them to jump ship. What was the effect of such evangelical theorization? The odds of chefs having all three of their signatures dishes in the nouvelle cuisine category go up 1,339 times as the number of pages devoted to theorization increases from 0 to 900.[18]

Moreover, the rebels promoting the nouvelle cuisine movement were not just peripheral individuals but chefs occupying legitimate positions of power in the professional society of French chefs. In 1969, the professional society of French chefs, Maîtres Queux et Cordons Bleus de France, was renamed Maîtres Cuisiniers de France (MCF), and its management consisted of four groups: founders and honorary presidents and vice presidents; an executive committee made up of an active president, three to five vice presidents, two general secretaries, two treasurers, and five to ten appointed members drawn from the ranks; an admission committee made up of twelve to eighteen members; and a control commission made up of three members. The first group and the control commission played marginal and cosmetic roles. Real power resided in the executive committee because it designed the agenda of the MCF, nominated members of the admissions committee, and thereby influenced admissions into the MCF. In turn, membership in the executive committee was by invitation, and the tradition was to invite recipients of three Michelin stars or winners of the Meilleur Ouvrier de France (MOF) titles.

Early nouvelle cuisine rebels such as Paul Bocuse, Jean Delaveyne, and Charles Barrier played key roles in the executive committee in the early years. These three chefs were winners of the prestigious MOF in 1961, 1952 and 1958, respectively, and were chefs in restaurants awarded three stars by the *Guide Michelin* in 1965, 1972, and 1968, respectively. By virtue of these accomplishments, they were welcomed into the executive committee because existing members believed that they would promote and develop the fading image of the MCF association. Over the years, newer nouvelle cuisine activists such as Alain Senderens and other nouvelle cuisine chefs who had worked as "seconds" to Bocuse, Delaveyne, and the others were also inducted into the executive committee, and in 1984, five of the six entrants to the executive committee were nouvelle cuisine exponents. After 1984, nouvelle cuisine activists and exponents steadily expanded control of the MCF board. As the proportion of nouvelle activists increased from zero to 10 percent, the odds of chefs adopting a nouvelle cuisine dish rose 2.29 times.

French chefs were also influenced by the defections of influential peers, that is, those with two or more Michelin stars who abandoned classical cuisine for nouvelle cuisine. Defections of visible peers are damaging because they are accessible and vivid and provide role models. Elite chefs realized that unlearning classical cuisine and embracing nouvelle cuisine was risky—it could undermine status—and paid keen attention to whether the adopters of nouvelle cuisine gained in reputations and Michelin stars as a result of their change. Chefs were attentive to the number of Michelin stars, desired more stars than they had, and were terrified of losing the ones that they possessed. Although the inspection by the *Guide Michelin* is performed anonymously and is opaque, chefs attributed a gain or loss of stars to changes in the menu and, by implication, the shift from classical to nouvelle cuisine. The odds of chefs having all three of their signature dishes in the nouvelle cuisine camp rose as the number of Michelin stars accruing to defectors rose.[19]

If collective action established nouvelle cuisine as a new style, how distinctive were its boundaries? Or were the boundaries undermined by innovation by chefs?

■ The Strength of the Boundary between Classical and Nouvelle Cuisine

Consider the L'Auberge de l'Ill, a restaurant run by the Haeberlin family in Alsace, France, which has been continuously awarded three stars by the *Guide Michelin* since 1970. But beneath this consistent quality, the nature of the signature dishes offered to patrons has undergone a remarkable series of changes. In 1970, a visitor to L'Auberge de l'Ill could select from pure classical cuisine signature dishes such as brioche de foie gras, salmon soufflé, and noisette de chevreuil Saint Hubert (venison). By 1980, pure nouvelle cuisine signature dishes such as salade de lapereau (young rabbit) had replaced some of the classical cuisine signature dishes on the menu. Thus, L'Auberge shifted from a purely classical cuisine French restaurant to a hybrid one that featured both classical and nouvelle cuisines. By 1995, the process of hybridization evolved further when the dishes themselves borrowed elements from both classical and nouvelle cuisines. In 1995, a patron could choose from ragoût de grenouilles poêlées, petit chou farci à la choucroute et aux grenouilles (fried frogs in stew, small cabbage stuffed with sauerkraut and frogs), and suprême de pigeonneau au chou en crépinettes, pastilla d'abats au foie d'oie (young pigeon with cabbage in crépinettes and giblets pastilla with goose liver). Stew and stuffed preparations are archetypal classical cuisine techniques, while suprême and crépinettes are nouvelle cuisine techniques. Pastilla and sauerkraut allude to the exotic influences of nouvelle cuisine, and the adjective "small" adds to the nuance, refinement, and diminutives typical of nouvelle cuisine.

This borrowing process blurred the boundaries between the two rival culinary categories, and the menus of many other elite French restaurants displayed the same pattern.

When did the heat that sustained the division between classical and nouvelle cuisine decline? Put another way, when did the boundaries between classical and nouvelle cuisine weaken, and how did this erosion occur? Interviews suggest that mixing and combining became more rampant during the late 1980s. François Simon, a journalist, described it as "the period of synthesis through the technique," and another Michelin inspector said that the rules of transgression had become "squared" or enhanced so that the boundaries between classical and nouvelle cuisine were becoming more ambiguous.[20]

How did it become cool to borrow and blend? Higher-status chefs, those with two or more stars, had more latitude to be original and could borrow from a rival category. Borrowing by high-status actors jump-started a process of borrowing by other actors such that lower-status chefs also began to borrow.[21] The odds of borrowing by a focal chef rose enormously as a result of high-status chefs' breaching boundaries.

■ Implications

The story of how rebels fueled the rise of nouvelle cuisine contains some important implications. New styles and new categories in cultural industries arise from oppositional identities fueled by collective action, but as the boundaries dissolve, new hybrid identities are created. Hip-hop, for instance, has thrived precisely because it, as a movement, affirmed an inner-city identity, espoused homophobia, and began as a reaction to the prevalent culture. However, the very success of hip-hop, especially rap, has led to the creation of new hybrid categories such as nu-metal, which blends hip-hop with rock and metal music.

The saga of nouvelle cuisine also reveals that attempts to create new styles and categories in cultural industries may fail when the the establishment begins to imitate the rebels, diluting their oppositional identity. Consider the Dogme movement in film, which sought to inveigh against Hollywood but was disarmed when many Hollywood directors started to embrace the Dogme critique.

On March 20, 1995, the Danish filmmaker Lars von Trier stood up at the Odeon Theatre in Paris—a key location in the May 1968 uprisings—on the one-hundredth anniversary of the cinema and tossed handfuls of pamphlets into the audience. Von Trier's "Dogme 95" portrayed films as a collective, impersonal effort and the introduction of digital technology as the ultimate democratization of the cinema, since anyone could then make movies. Since the tricks and the movie cosmetics of Hollywood created an illusion of pathos and love and did not communicate emotions, Dogme 95 set out to counter the film of illusion by presenting an indisputable set of rules known as the Vows of Chastity, which prescribed shooting on location with a handheld camera, forbade easy plots (for example, no murders and no guns), precluded temporal and geographical alienation (the film has to take place now and here), and inveighed against artificial props and sets on location, special lighting, optical work, filters, and music (unless any of these occurred where the scene was being shot). Finally, the director could not be credited.

In the United States, Dogme was perceived as a low-budget, independent method of filmmaking that did not attract establishment artists like Francis Ford Coppola or Martin Scorsese (themselves products of an earlier independent movement) nor the American independent scene, such as the Sundance Film Festival. To spread the Dogme gospel, von Trier and Thomas Vinterberg set up an association, Dogme Brothers, which would provide training to new Dogme directors, starting with seminars in Argentina. However, over time Dogme slowly became a "brand." In the United States more than a dozen directors began planning to shoot a Dogme film. In October 1999, at the Universal Pictures Film Conference, Steven Spielberg spoke enthusiastically about Dogme and announced his intention to make a Dogme film. Martin Scorsese called von Trier a "wonderful film-maker . . . who got furious, threw everything up in the air, and said, Look, let's start from nowhere now."[22]

In August 2002, Lars von Trier and his three co-signatories of the Dogme 95 manifesto—Vinterberg, Søren Kragh-Jacobsen, and Kristian Levring—issued a statement saying they were "alarmed by the success of their revolutionary method of film-making" and had decided that they would no longer authorize new Dogme films. The three wanted to prevent Dogme from "becoming a commercial concept used to market movies rather than a creative principle used to redefine film-making." According to Vinterberg, Dogme died because it had been "accepted and corrupted" and "the whole idea was to create renewal. Dogme had become bourgeois."[23] For his part, von Trier suggested that "the more fashionable Dogme had become, the more boring."[24]

Collective action can undermine conventions and create genres or styles, and it can also set in motion a collision between the irresistible force of culture and the immovable object of business. A telling example is the free-music movement, which celebrates the free sharing of songs on the basis of peer-to-peer (P2P) sharing of digital files, fueled by Napster, Kazaa, and other file-sharing Web sites. The recording industry has responded with a strategy of litigation, but another counteroffensive has been created wherein universities seek to offer legal file-sharing services as an alternative. Cable providers have been trying to develop tiered pricing structures that link price to bandwidth speed in a bid to broaden their market and not necessarily to limit song-swapping. Nevertheless, such tiered pricing can also impede the free-music movement.

■

The previous chapters have shown that social movements play a crucial role in promoting radical technological innovations that create new markets, open up new niches, or herald new styles in cultural industries. But what about radical administrative innovations that transform governance in markets and radically alter the distribution of power between stakeholders in an enterprise? In the next chapter, I turn the attention to capital markets and how rebels seeking to protect investor rights introduced new arrangements that altered the distribution of power between shareholders and executives in America, arrangements which then spread to Germany.

Show Me the Money
Shareholder Activism and Investor Rights

Robert Nardelli, the former CEO of Home Depot, received $245 million in compensation from the board from 2000 until 2005, when the stock slid by 12 percent despite the $20.3 billion stock buyback program. During the same time period, Lowe's, Home Depot's rival, saw its stock go up by 173 percent. In 2005, even when Home Depot's stock was stagnant, the board raised Nardelli's salary by 8 percent to $2.16 million and boosted his bonus by 22 percent to $7 million. In dramatic contrast, Lowe's CEO, Robert Tillman, was given less than a quarter of what Nardelli received.[1] Outraged Home Depot shareholder activists put a number of anti-management resolutions to a vote and demanded greater oversight of executive pay and retirement benefits, as well as changes in the election of directors. In a bid to shame directors into addressing the bleak situation, activist investors targeted ten out of the eleven directors and asked shareholders to "vote no" on their election as a symbolic protest.

Instead of the usual venue, Atlanta, the annual general meeting of shareholders occurred in Wilmington, Delaware. Nardelli attended the meeting, but none of the directors did. Only fifty shareholders showed, and the meeting was Webcast in New York. Outside the meeting, protesters carried placards reviling Nardelli as "OCEO" ("Overpaid CEO") and exhorted shareholders to vote for the resolutions (see figure

Figure 5.1
Protest outside
the Home Depot
shareholder
meeting, 2006.
William Thomas
Cain/Getty
Images.

5.1). Even though the turnout was small, the protesters were able to gain coverage in the media and sustain a drumbeat of criticism that eventually led to Nardelli's exit.

Indeed, the only shareholder-sponsored resolution that passed was the one demanding board changes in elections. The meeting lasted thirty minutes, and the few shareholders were given exactly one minute to ask a question. Ten of the eleven targeted directors received symbolic "no votes" from shareholders (the directors who received the highest number of votes still only garnered 30 to 36 percent of the votes, thereby revealing shareholder dissatisfaction). The cavalier treatment of shareholders fueled investor discontent. One institutional investor, Relational Investors, wanted an independent evaluation of the firm's direction at the next meeting, and New York City's Employees Retirement System and other public pension funds vowed to organize a proxy fight. On January 3, 2007, Nardelli resigned after purportedly rejecting a suggestion to take a pay cut.

The effort to enforce shareholder rights at Home Depot was not an isolated incident but part of a larger investor rights movement whose origins can be traced back to 1947. It was in 1947 that John and Lewis Gilbert, two rebellious shareholders, asked Transamerica management to add a resolution on the use of outside auditors in the proxy statement, but Transamerica managers declined. The Securities and Exchange Commission (SEC) entered the fray on the side of the Gilbert brothers, and eventually the appeals court ruled that the managers could not exclude such a resolution. This case provided a legal basis for the right of shareholders to file shareholder-sponsored resolutions.

Pioneers that they were, the Gilbert brothers and another prominent rebel, Evelyn Davis, were lonely sentries in the ramparts of shareholder rights and shareholder value from the 1950s until the late 1980s. Davis, who later proclaimed herself the "Queen of the Corporate Jungle," would immobilize CEOs in shareholder meetings with her antics (she once paraded in a bathing suit in a 1970 General Motors meeting), her rhetoric (she reviled the "Nazi tactics" of one CEO), and her persistence. Other than these gadflies, who served stinging criticism and annoyed managers, there was hardly anyone else interested in shareholder rights. Indeed, between the 1960s and the 1980s, the shareholder resolution pioneered by the Gilbert brothers became the stick with which Ralph Nader, Saul Alinsky, and the Interfaith Center for Corporate Responsibility beat corporate managers to instill social responsibility into the conduct of multinational corporations under the influence of the civil rights movement and the environmental movement.

How did persistent activism by isolated rebels snowball into a social movement that had investor rights at the forefront of its agenda in the United States? Investor rights was made into a *hot cause* and anti-management campaigns were transformed into a source of *cool mobilization*. Gadflies, institutional investors, and mutual fund activists all played complementary roles, and the anti-management shareholder resolution was supplemented by other tools of cool mobilization, including corporate blacklists and vote-no campaigns designed to shame directors.

■ **Investor Rights and Anti-Management Campaigns**

The literature on corporate governance has traditionally assumed an efficiency-oriented approach, first heralded by Adolphe Berle and Gardner Means. A striking example of the efficiency emphasis is the agency theory view of the firm, which takes the separation of ownership from management as the starting point. According to agency theory, a firm is a nexus of contracts between multiple stakeholders with conflicting interests, and there is an inherent agency problem since the interests of the agents (i.e., managers) are not completely aligned with the interests of the principals (i.e., shareholders). As a result, there may be a divergence of interests between managers and shareholders, leading managers to promote their own goals at the expense of those of the shareholders, unless incentive mechanisms and monitoring mechanisms (e.g., the board of directors, the market for takeovers) are designed.[2]

From this perspective, shareholder activism as a rational attempt to discipline management and shareholder resolutions can be conceptualized as a mechanism that aligns managerial behaviors with shareholder interests by changing the bylaws governing management's activities. But such a portrait does not answer many questions: Why did shareholder activism emerge in the mid-1980s and not earlier? Since about one in three proposed resolutions actually gains majority support among shareholders, and even then has only weak effects on corporate performance, why do activists rely on them? Shareholder activism was an outgrowth of a social movement dedicated to investor rights. Below I will demonstrate how shareholder resolutions are a form of symbolic protest behavior.

Social movements arise when there is a political opportunity, available mobilization structures, and frames that articulate grievances and proffer solutions.[3] The investor rights movement was stoked by a political opportunity spawned by the rise of the institutional investor, forums of collective action, ready-made grievances, and the redeployment of an old tool of mobilization—the anti-management resolution pioneered by the Gilberts.

As the proportion of an average firm's equity controlled by institutional investors such as banks, insurance firms, investment companies, mutual funds, and public pension funds rose from 15.8 percent in 1965 to 42.7 percent in 1986, ownership of the modern corporation shifted from individual investors to large organizations. Investors with a larger number of shares have higher exit costs—large-scale selling of shares depresses stock prices. So divestment became costly and activism became more appealing. Private pension funds, banks, and mutual funds were beholden to the managers of business firms and had little incentive to discipline them. In contrast, public pension funds were not captives of managers and were compelled by the Employee Retirement Income Security Act (ERISA) to discharge their fiduciary responsibilities to their constituents. Public pension fund managers realized that the takeovers market could not discipline managers, and turned to political oversight and activism to check errant managers.

A growing wave of takeovers in the 1980s aggravated the conflict between managers of firms and their investors. During the 1980s, 29 percent of the Fortune 500 industrial firms were targets of takeover attempts by outsiders. Takeovers tended to benefit shareholders by increasing stock prices but jeopardized the interests of managers. Managers sought to defend themselves through "shark repellents," "poison pills" (mechanisms that depressed share prices and reduced shareholder discretion), "golden parachutes" (handsome pay packages to executives fired in takeovers), and "greenmail" (buying back raiders' shares at a high premium while leaving other shareholders disadvantaged). The takeover controversies spawned innumerable congressional hearings, and sixty bills to regulate takeovers were introduced between 1984 and 1987. No new legislation saw light because of the Reagan administration's opposition and the disinterested attitude of the SEC.

Public pension funds such as CalPERS (the California Public Employees Retirement Systems) and the California State Teachers Retirement Fund were leading the wave of organizational rebellion. A watershed event was the creation of the Council of Institutional Investors (CII) in January 1985. In 1986, CII endorsed a shareholder bill of rights that asked for shareholder approval for greenmail, poison pills, golden parachutes, and issuance of excessive debt. Its underlying principle was that informed shareholders should have the right to approve fundamental corporate actions to a degree that is proportional to their invested capital at risk. Other public pension funds such as TIAA-CREF also began to articulate shareholders' grievances and presented the exercise of voting rights as the solution to curtail the power of errant corporate managers. National organizations such as the National Council of Public Employee Retirement Systems and the National Association of State Retirement Administrators provided the social infrastructure for the investor rights movement. Thus, the circle of market rebels widened.

The SEC's Rule 14a-8 allows shareholders to sponsor resolutions challenging managers at annual meetings and therefore is an institutionally provided channel of voice. A favored strategy by which investor rights activists such as TIAA-CREF sought to pressure managers to accept expanded shareholder rights was to bring governance-related resolutions challenging the management of errant companies. Typically, such resolutions offered a rival slate of directors or asked shareholders to disapprove management proposals deemed inimical to shareholders' interests. Such anti-management resolutions were attempts by investor rights activists to browbeat managers into recognizing shareholders' rights to receive information, influence fundamental business decisions, and set acceptable levels of performance. In 1990 alone, more shareholder proposals passed than "in the entire history of shareholder proposals prior to 1990."[4] Activists submitted 307 proposals in 1994, and by 2003 the number had shot up to 723.[5]

■ **Anti-Management Resolutions**
   as Sources of Cool Mobilization

Institutional investors such as public pension funds prefer "less public forms of activism such as private letters and phone calls to management. . . . Thus, in many instances filing a proposal on the proxy statement became unnecessary and was used only as a 'last resort.'"[6] Usually, "when an institution has an issue it is concerned about, it typically will contact a firm privately about the issue first. Depending on the firm's response, the institution will determine whether to file a proxy resolution."[7] If shareholder-sponsored anti-management resolutions are an avenue of last resort, they signal a breakdown in the negotiation process between institutional investors and management.

So who files the bulk of anti-management resolutions? Gadflies—persons "habitually engaged in provocative criticism of existing institutions" and who lack access to informal channels of negotiation.[8] Unlike religious groups who mainly focus on social issues and corporate social responsibility, these rebels focus on corporate governance issues. Gadflies also share a common identity as rebels—an identity created by managers. Gadflies are generally lumped together and discussed as vocal, persistent activists by managers and the media. Robert Monks, a gadfly himself, described the role of gadflies thus:

> Okay, then you have a few people who are charitably described as gadflies, in which category I might fit. We're not the straw that stirs this soda. We can every once in a while get people's attention, but we don't stir this soda. So the hell of it is that in the existing system, without having the declaration of a federal policy of shareholder activism, the only owners who are actively involved are marginal. I don't like thinking of myself as being marginal, but "them's the facts." Where are the great and the good? Where are the people who ought to be doing something here? Who's the largest shareholder? . . . There has never been an occasion of involvement in activism by an ERISA plan. Never. Not one. The IBM pension plan has never been involved. At the moment, what we are talking about is a fringe activity and it isn't fringe because we are fringe people; it's fringe because nobody else finds it convenient to join us.[9]

Early evidence suggested that only a fraction of the antimanagement shareholder resolutions garner support, and most of the resolutions initiated by gadflies fail to do so. Most such studies found that shareholder resolutions had no effect on policy changes or performance, and the ones that did depended on the issue and the success of the negotiation.[10] A recent study suggests that in the post-Enron environment, there has been a marked increase in the propensity to implement non-binding resolutions that received majority support: in 1997, only 16 percent of such resolutions were implemented. In 2003, 40 percent of them were implemented, especially when peer industry firms also implemented similar proposals.[11]

Rebels expend time and effort to propose resolutions that don't generate change or discernibly improve performance because these are symbolic protests—disruptive acts that "cannot reasonably be expected to end the injustice, to prevent its recurrence, or to rectify it in any way."[12] Symbolic protests are a means to inspire the target base and focalize the struggle between the threatening "they" (the management) and the threatened "we" (small shareholders).[13]

In fact, "most activist shareholders don't expect to win; what they realistically—and appropriately—hope for is the chance to air their points of view."[14] Therefore, while shareholder proposals are rarely passed, gadflies rely on the fact that firms may be weary of "taking actions that have led to expressions of shareholder disapproval at other companies."[15] Consider how Evelyn Davis filed proposals asking that staggered boards be replaced by annual elections to Bristol-Myers Squibb; it was only after six straight years, when her proposal finally garnered more than 60 percent of the vote, that management decided to abandon staggered board elections for annual elections. Thus, John Gilbert donned a red clown nose to shareholder meetings, and Evelyn Davis chided Lee Iacocca of Chrysler about his diet. As the Bristol-Myers example reveals, shareholder resolutions seek to create publicity.

More generally, investor rights gadflies target visible firms—larger firms are more vulnerable to criticism, easier to symbolize as the enemy, and garner the most publicity. Social activists target firms for their "size and prestige" rather than only their acts of commission. Thus, the Project on Corporate Responsibility (PCR), an environmental watch-dog, targeted General Motors to draw national attention, and the Coalition for Environmentally Responsible Economies (CERES) targeted Amoco to put their respective agendas on the public's table—not because they expected to generate changes.

Large organizations are often the most visible: "Large firms constitute better targets because more shareholder wealth can be created if they respond to . . . pressures and be-cause their reaction is more likely to have an impact on other firms in the industry." Poor performance also provides unin-tended visibility for firms; for example, firms that were tar-geted by the United Shareholders Association significantly underperformed the market and their industries. Poor per-formance, as in the Home Depot episode, heightens visibility and precipitates action. Improvements in performance re-duce the probability of a shareholder resolution by as much as 8 percent.[16] Attention is also easily acquired through "lightning rod" issues. Sociological research on protests suggests that latent grievances may be suddenly realized through lightning rod issues that precipitate action.[17] For example, flawed prisoner executions outraged public sensibilities and enabled opponents of capital punishment to ban the death penalty in some states. Typically, lightning rod issues create a shock effect and provide emotional intensification of grievances.

In the context of corporations, executive compensation has become a lightning rod issue. Huge compensation—like Robert Nardelli's $245 million—garners media attention, fuels questioning and controversy, and eventually stokes feelings of indignation and outrage. High executive compensation rallies shareholders, crystallizes latent opposition, makes it easier for activists to exploit the "us" versus "them" mind-set, and triggers collective action. However, high levels of executive compensation do not increase the overall number of resolutions. Instead, it provides an impetus for shareholder resolutions designed to remove staggered board elections and create annual elections, thereby lowering the degree to which executives are able to entrench themselves by having allies on the board. Each one-unit increment in salary enhances the likelihood of a resolution demanding board declassification and the initiation of annual elections by 400 percent.[18]

■ Playing Defense: Investor Relations Departments

Shareholders have existed since the formation of the joint-stock corporation. Investor relations departments that view investors as "customers" and market a "story" are of a more recent vintage. One case study of seven organizations revealed:

> Until the 1980s, to the extent that shareholders occupied management time at all, investor relations was often the province of the chief financial officer (CFO). As shareholders' questions would periodically arise, the CFO would take time from a full schedule to respond. Investor relations then entailed little more than public relations and occasional crisis management. . . . At decade's end, by contrast, the investor relations office had become a full-time professionalized operation. . . . The investor relations manager occupied an office proximate to, if not within, the executive suite in all seven companies.[19]

Firms responded to pressure from shareholders by establishing special-purpose investor relations (IR) departments to contain investor dissent. The creation of special departments to manage investor relations enabled top managers to signal their commitment to investor rights. Because interpretations of whether or not corporate decisions favor investors are complex, given potential conflicts between short-term and long-term performance, top managers found it rational to hire personnel to buffer themselves from external scrutiny. IR departments also gave top managers an infrastructure for "educating" shareholders and analysts, attracting certain types of investors and retaining them as long-term partners.

Essentially, these departments provide a mechanism through which firms can "educate" investors and persuade them that the company is responsive to their concerns. One study found that the propensity of firms to create IR departments rose as the number of anti-management investor resolutions increased throughout the early phases of the shareholder rights movement. The impact of the institutional variables is striking.

IR departments also spread through board interlocks among the Fortune 500 companies. Communication with contacts diminishes ambiguity about the value of an innovation and promotes vicarious learning from the experiences of others. Board interlocks connect a focal organization with other organizations and structurally embed it in an intercorporate network. A number of studies show that board interlocks serve as conduits for the transmission of information and norms about what is desirable and what is appropriate. Board interlocks with prior adopters (a situation in which a director of a board sits on the board of another firm that has already adopted an innovation or practice) also have strong effects: each interlock increases the presence of IR departments by 12 percent.

Did IR departments enable firms to tamp down shareholder protests? Often, boundary-spanning units like the Equal Employment Office (EEO) are thought to reduce the number of complaints, but they actually wind up increasing complaints because the presence of such an office signals commitment to equal rights, and also because office staff may encourage employees to pursue those rights.[20] Similarly, IR departments served as magnets to attract shareholder protests—the presence of such an office increased the probability of shareholder protests by 71 percent.[21]

■ Cool Mobilization through Vote-No Campaigns

A recent innovation in the investor rights movement is the vote-no campaign. In virtually all states directors are elected by plurality, that is, by winning the most votes in an election. When elections are uncontested, a director can win an election if he or she receives just one vote. In 1993, Joseph Grundfest, a former chairman of the SEC and a law professor, suggested that when shareholders withhold votes, it amounts to a vote of no confidence against individual directors that besmirches their reputations and compels them to respond.[22] For example, activist shareholders launched a vote-no campaign against the CEO of Disney, Michael Eisner, and George Mitchell, a director. The former had 45 percent of votes withheld and the latter 26 percent. Eisner resigned the next day, only to be replaced by Mitchell.

Since 1993, more than 150 vote-no campaigns have been launched, and public pension funds have taken the baton from gadfly investors and now sponsor more than half of all the vote-no campaigns, typically targeting individual directors rather than the entire slate.[23] Vote-no campaigns are initiated when a firm suffers from poor performance and management has cavalierly refused to implement a shareholder proposal that has secured majority support. In the Home Depot example, shareholders were incensed that Home Depot directors had refused to implement a proposal calling for shareholder oversight of severance benefits for top managers, and in 2006 they launched a vote-no campaign against ten of the eleven directors. Thirty-one to 36 percent of the votes were withheld—some of the highest percentages ever recorded. Another striking example is Safeway. In 2004, four public pension funds targeted Safeway for a vote-no campaign—generating withheld votes of 15 to 17 percent against CEO Steve Burd and two directors. As a result of the campaign, Safeway introduced a number of governance changes, including naming an independent lead director.

A recent study suggests that vote-no campaigns improve governance practices and finds that directors specifically targeted in vote-no campaigns lose, on average, one or more public company directorships than directors at these same firms who were not targeted by name. The penalties for directors are even more stringent when the vote-no campaigns impugn the directors' fidelity and ability, as when they sit on the compensation committee and approve disproportionately large pay packages for CEOs.[24]

A number of scandals—including Enron, where internal incentives for managers distorted decisions and led to a tragic debacle, and Tyco, where CEO Dennis Kozlowski lived an opulent life at the expense of shareholders—have fueled the growth of the vote-no campaigns. Scandals create human-interest stories that facilitate media placement and generate scenes and personae that audiences feel they know and identify with. Moreover, scandals also initiate a narrative arc and maintain public interest and outrage, and they create a discursive space for moral issues to be debated and provoke active involvement by the public.

One barometer of the investor rights movement's growth is the number of shareholder proposals. In 2002 alone, 802 proposals were brought to vote, and in 2003 the number shot up to 1,082. In the first half of 2004, there were

1,147 proposals on the anvil according to the Investor Responsibility Research Center.

A more important but delayed consequence was that the scandals, in conjunction with the vote-no campaign, led to a concerted effort to institute majority voting for the election of directors. Under majority voting, directors are required to receive a majority of votes cast, and the failure to receive majority support would trigger board action. In 2005, the Council of Institutional Investors orchestrated a letter-writing campaign to 1,500 of the largest U.S. corporations exhorting them to adopt majority voting rules for directors. In June 2005, Pfizer amended its corporate governance procedures such that directors who fail to receive the affirmative majority of votes in an uncontested election must submit their resignation to the Corporate Governance Committee of the Pfizer board, and the board would decide within ninety days whether to accept or reject the resignation. More than 150 companies, including Microsoft and Johnson & Johnson, have adopted similar principles. By contrast, Intel has developed a different model: they amended the corporate bylaws to provide for a majority voting standard in uncontested elections. Bylaws are more difficult to change than governance procedures, but even then, some activists want majority approval of shareholders for any changes in bylaws. The Intel model has been hailed as a gold standard by proxy advisory firms, and forty-five firms, including Dell, Clear Channel, and even Home Depot, have adopted this standard.

Although institutional activists such as public pension funds have played a valuable role in promoting shareholder rights, it is also important to recognize that such activists may have conflicts with other shareholders. While it is true that there is a conflict of interest between managers and shareholders because of the separation of control, there may also be a potential conflict of interest between portfolio investors seeking to advance their social agendas and other investors. An interesting study distinguishes between governance-related activism and the social activism of CalPERS, the largest public pension fund in the United States, which has a Focus List in which it targets companies for poor performance, egregious governance, and unfair compensation practices. It started publicly announcing which firms were on the Focus List from 1992 onward and has identified 115 firms. Such announcements constitute one form of governance-related activism, and there has been a positive reaction from the stock market on the days that the Focus List is announced—on average 23 basis points, amounting to $224 million annually, or $3.1 billion over the period of the study from 1992 to 2005. By contrast, the social activism of CalPERS, such as divesting from tobacco firms and so forth, did not enhance shareholder wealth.

- **The Cross-National Diffusion of the Investor Rights Movement: Germany**

The investor rights movement has spread from the United States to a number of countries, including Germany, France, Sweden, and Japan. The original German law of 1937 holds that a firm should be run for the welfare of the enterprise and its employees, the citizens, and the state. German banks have historically played a key role as financial intermediaries and as sources of finance to firms, and also as shareholders. Germany does not allow class actions, which constrains small shareholders from pooling their resources.

Political opportunity for a shareholder rights movement began as a result of a number of factors. One was that German CEOs centrally located in the intercorporate network began using the logic of shareholder value either to change strategy (as in Daimler-Benz, then Daimler-Chrysler, now just Daimler again), to demonstrate to critics that disinvestment was not needed (as in Bayer), or to launch takeovers to enhance performance (as in Krupp). The growth in the number of firms claiming adherence to shareholder value rose. A second factor was that the clubby cohesion among banks and firms began to give way as banks began to pursue investment banking and Deutsche Bank supported a hostile takeover in a firm where it had a representative on the supervisory board. The surge in privatization of publicly owned firms such as Deutsche Telekom (the People's Stock) also meant that the number of people who own stocks or mutual funds has more than doubled since 1997 to 12.3 million, according to the German Share Institute. Only 433 firms were listed on the market in 1983, but an explosion of public offerings meant that the number rose to 933 by the end of the 1990s. Moreover, the Liberal Party in the German government pushed for the Corporate Sector Supervision and Transparency Act (KonTraG), which put in place the one-share, one-vote rule, and replaced the 1937 law's emphasis on stakeholders with a new emphasis on shareholders. A German government Commission on Corporate Governance also mandated voluntary new standards of transparency and compliance.

New mobilization structures also arose. Two new associations, the DSW (German Security Holders' Protection Association) and SdK (Capital Investors Protection Association), have spearheaded shareholder rights. Although founded in 1947 as the national headquarters of investment clubs, the DSW now has 28,000 members and serves as a watchdog, opposing proposals of management and demanding the adoption of transparency and accountability in corporate governance. Its smaller counterpart, the SdK, performs similar functions. Activist investors from the United States have also served as role models for German investors, some of whom have emigrated from other countries. For example, Guy Wyser Pratt, referred to by the German media as "Rambo der Kapitalmarkte," became infamous when he told German and European elites managing firms to "wake up and smell the napalm." One of his early successes in Germany was to orchestrate a campaign against the IWKA, the German industrial machinery maker; he was able to persuade 38 percent of the shareholders to withhold approval of the board, and forced the CEO to resign.

Scandals have become lightning rod issues that have fueled shareholder opposition to corporate managers. In recent years, the scandal over a 420 million Euro slush fund that enabled Siemens to get contracts precipitated dissatisfaction over performance, which induced the SdK to lead an effort to withhold approval of board members and call for the resignation of its chairman. A similar scandal at Volkswagen over the squandering of millions of Euros by executives, union officials, and politicians also led to an intensification of shareholder opposition. Both scandals have led to a renewed call for transparency about executive pay, especially in the thirty largest German companies.

What has been diffusing into the German business environment is not only the ideology of shareholder value but also shareholder tactics such as withholding approval and the targeting of poorly performing firms by the DSW and SdK. Shareholder activists have been challenging the ascension of former CEOs to the role of chairman of the supervisory board, and there is a drive to make such a move legally impossible.

■ Implications

Fifty years ago, in *The Solid Gold Cadillac*, first staged as a play and then filmed as a movie, Laura Partridge (played by Judy Halliday in the film), a small shareholder owning ten shares, attends a meeting of the General Products Corporation in which the directors have awarded themselves huge compensation, and asks a series of embarrassing questions. In a bid to squelch her, the directors employ Laura as the director of shareholder relations but find to their surprise that she orchestrates a shareholder revolt, and is eventually awarded a solid gold Cadillac for her activism.

Both the play and the movie were far ahead of their time. It took more than thirty years for the shareholder rights movement to emerge in the United States and for activists to be able to successfully demand changes in corporate governance. Unlike other movements described in this book, the shareholder rights movement decisively reshaped the market for corporate control and the market for directors. It then spread to Germany—a locale that one would have thought would be hostile to the ideology of shareholder value, given its historical disregard for shareholder value.

The staple tactics of shareholders, to use the vocabulary of economist Albert Hirschman, was not to exit the organization but to exercise "voice" by filing shareholder resolutions or withholding votes. Such symbolic actions play an important part in the functioning of power—power is not merely the control of resources but also pertains to the ability to frame awareness and attention. For marginal actors, power is based on their ability to use symbolic actions to embarrass, shame, and prod their more powerful opponents into making concessions and initiating changes.

A striking implication of this chapter is that a prosaic setting like the annual general meeting of shareholders can be an arena for rebellion and movement activity. While there is a dichotomy between studying disruptive movement politics on the one hand, and institutional procedures that encourage accommodative action on the other, institutionalized spaces are habitats where activists disrupt work and draw attention to favorite issues. For example, the Women Military Aviators served as a habitat in which feminists could become active and initiate change within the U.S. military, and religious orders within the Catholic Church served as similar habitats for feminists campaigning for change. Institutionalized channels in the SEC provide an arena for social movements to alter the market for corporate control.

In the negotiated relationship between management and shareholders, shareholder activism is more than incidental friction and a fundamental challenge for managers. Managers engage in a variety of window-dressing behaviors to respond to shareholder activism, including the implementation of long-term plans and stock buybacks. But as this chapter shows, unintended consequences can ensue from window dressing—so attempts to establish investor relations departments to contain shareholder dissent boomeranged and instead increased the number of anti-management shareholder resolutions. It was the very same lesson that the executives of the General Products Corporation in *The Solid Gold Cadillac* learned when they employed Laura Partridge as the director of shareholder relations.

■

The previous chapters chronicle how collective action by activists promotes radical business innovation by creating new markets as in the case of gasoline-powered cars, promoting new niches in mature markets such as beer, spawning radical technological change in creative industries such as gastronomy, and promoting new governance arrangements that altered the distribution of power between shareholders and managers in capital markets. But social movements may also arise to impede radical business innovation by curtailing new entrants that embody new technologies and preventing the commercialization of technology by large firms that already possess the capabilities to do so. I explore these dynamics in the succeeding chapters. I first turn to the dance between incumbents and invaders and discuss how activists attempted to protect small businesses in the retail sector from the attack by chain stores in the 1920s in America by launching a grassroots movement that pressured legislators to enact laws hostile to chain stores—and how, in turn, chain stores fought back.

Chain Reaction
The Enactment and Repeal of Anti–Chain Store Laws

From 1990 to 2000, the retail sector in the United States experienced an extraordinary degree of consolidation. Eleven thousand independent pharmacies closed during that period. Independent bookstores accounted for 58 percent of book sales in 1972 but only 17 percent of book sales in 2000. Two hardware chains captured 30 percent of the market by 2000. In 1995, five firms controlled 19 percent of the grocery market, and by 2000 their share reached 33 percent. The growth of large chains or "big box" stores has ignited a social movement seeking to preserve the identities of small towns and to protect small businesses.

Wal-Mart, which at one time opened two stores every day—and which accounted for 7 percent of all consumer spending in 2000—is a prototype par excellence of how chain store expansion has met with resistance and how collective action designed to protect local identities is fueled. In 1993, the town leaders of Greenfield, Massachusetts, a 240-year-old factory town ninety miles northwest of Boston, approved a Wal-Mart proposal to rezone industrial land into commercial land and transform a 63-acre lot into a store of 120,000 square feet that would pay $100,000 in taxes. A number of anti-Wal-Mart groups sprang up, and Al Norman, a resident of Greenfield, sparked a campaign that emphasized the loss of a small-town feel and the demise of local businesses. As he put it, "There's one thing you can't buy in a Wal-Mart—that's small-town quality of life. And once you lose it, you can't get it back at any price."[1]

A "We are against the Wal Committee" was organized and the anti-Wal-Mart campaign peppered the town with lawn signs and bumper stickers saying that the store was so large it could easily accommodate three baseball stadiums the size of Boston's Fenway Park. Two town referenda were held, and in both cases voters turned down the proposal. A key factor influencing voters was an independent study paid for by Wal-Mart, which forecasted that the store would turn 65 percent of competing retail space in Franklin County into vacancies, that it would reduce Greenfield's commercial property values by 33 percent, and that it would create essentially no net gains in either jobs or property taxes. Soon two other nearby communities followed suit and rejected Wal-Mart's plans.

Nationwide, an anti–chain store movement dedicated to containing the expansion of big box stores has mushroomed, and stores like Home Depot and Rite Aid have been seared by public protests. After the Greenfield campaign, Al Norman organized a protest group called the Sprawl Busters to defeat big box initiatives, and a number of other protest groups have also emerged. As of October 2006, 309 communities had rebuffed the expansion plans of big box retailers.

The movement against big box stores that started in the early 1990s is reminiscent of an earlier popular upsurge against retail chain stores in America. Starting in the 1920s, chains like A&P and Montgomery Ward proliferated across the countryside and transformed the retail sector. The expansion of retail chain stores evoked social debate and contention in schools and colleges regarding the loss of identity. For instance, on December 12, 1929, the Ohio State University debating team defeated Northwestern University on the resolution "That the principle of the chain store system is detrimental to the best interests of the US public."[2] In 1930, 500 college and high school debates focused on the same topic; clearly, something was afoot. By 1931, there were 5,000 debates presented before 1.9 million attendees. Both anti–chain store and pro–chain store forces prepared debate manuals listing talking points for the debates and distributed them widely.[3]

The debate about chain stores was not confined to college campuses but spilled over into the legislatures and courts. For instance, in 1929, the state of Indiana instituted a chain store tax under which the first store paid the state $3 per year, the next four paid $10, the next five $15, the next ten $20, and all above that $25. The owner of a grocery chain of 225 stores, Lafayette Jackson, filed a suit in the U.S. Supreme Court on the grounds of discrimination because he was taxed $5,443 as compared to $675 for the same number of individual stores, but he lost his appeal in 1931. Between 1931 and 1939 twenty-seven of the forty-eight U.S. states passed such laws, and in 1938, nineteen were active. After 1938, the legislative tide against chains turned, and a number of anti-chain laws were repealed because pro–chain store forces petitioned the Supreme Court to declare the state tax laws illegal and unconstitutional.

What underlay the contention over the role of chain stores and the enactment and repeal of anti–chain store laws? Market rebels rely on "non-market" strategies such as the enactment of laws to restrict the entry of larger and more powerful firms into existing markets. The enactment of anti–chain store tax laws is also a striking illustration of how market rebels seek to protect local traditions and identities from the onslaught of large and powerful corporations. I focus on the anti–chain store episode in the 1920s because it provides a historical context to appreciate the unfolding social drama about the expansion of the big box stores today.

As chain stores became dominant in American life, an anti–chain store movement seeking to protect small businessmen and the mom-and-pop retail store emerged. Its chief tactic was to pressure legislators into enacting laws designed to punitively tax chain stores. By contrast, as the anti–chain store movement gained steam, pro–chain store forces also organized themselves into a trade association and mounted a counterattack to roll back these laws. In what follows I will elaborate the tussle between the anti–chain store movement and the pro–chain store forces and show how anti–chain store activists championed the *hot cause* of small business and sought to protect them with a form of *cool mobilization*.[4]

■ Mom-and-Pop Stores and Punitive Taxes

The motivation for opposition to chains stemmed from their rapid rise in the 1920s. Estimates of the number of chain stores in 1920 range from 27,000 to 50,000, while the 1929 census of retailing counted 141,492.[5] This increase prompted a resolution calling for a chain-store inquiry by the Federal Trade Commission, which was introduced to the U.S. Senate in 1928 by Smith Brookhart of Iowa. But the earliest anti-chain efforts came from the wholesalers and retailers who were most affected by the growth of chain stores. In the early 1920s, wholesalers in the grocery industry pressured manufacturers not to sell directly to chains. Orders by the Federal Trade Commission to desist such practices in Texas (1922), California (1924), and Arkansas (1924) curtailed this type of pressure.

Later in the 1920s, the anti-chain opposition took on a grassroots character, expressing itself in myriad forms all over the country. By 1929 "trade-at-home" advertising campaigns existed in more than four hundred communities. For example, in Springfield, Missouri, the local chamber of commerce launched a campaign with the slogan "Keep Ozark Dollars in the Ozarks." Advertisements in the *Springfield Leader* claimed that chain store managers were "mechanical operators" whose duties were to "get Springfield's money and to send it to the Home Office."[6]

The opponents of chains also exploited emerging mass media to broadcast their message. W. K. ("Old Man") Henderson, the owner and operator of KWKH radio (the K standing for "Kennonball") in Shreveport, Louisiana, inveighed against chains, labeling them "chain gang interests." In the Pacific Northwest, Montaville Flowers attacked chains in a series of thirty-six half-hour broadcasts.[7] "Fighting" Bob Duncan broadcast his attacks from a small station in Portland, which in 1931 became the first community in the country to pass a municipal anti-chain law. The anti–chain store message was also popularized by movies, including *Helping Grandma* (1931), which featured the Little Rascals helping Grandma, the owner of a tiny general store, scare off representatives of a chain store seeking to buy her out.

The muckraking film *Forward America*, made by Frank Wilson (foreshadowing the genre of contemporary films exposing firms, such as *Wal-Mart* by Robert Greenwald or any of Michael Moore's movies), also had substantial impact. Throughout the country, independent businesspeople bought twenty-five-cent tickets and distributed them to their customers. Eventually pro-chain forces stopped the practice by claiming it was a violation of National Recovery Act codes against false advertising. The film was billed as "an unequaled exposé" featuring "startling" and sensational facts about chain stores.

The message communicated through these channels was clear: the independent businessperson, threatened by the chains, was an integral part of U.S. democracy. In 1936 the National Association of Retail Druggists described chains as representing the "privilege-seeking few [who] seek . . . the dictatorship of big money—a state of financial feudalism . . . privilege-seeking tycoons . . . would-be dictators" and declared, "The selfishness of those who would control the money power of the nation, if their greed is allowed to develop unchecked . . . [would leave] masses of Americans wholly at the mercy of the despotic power of a monopolistic class."[8]

The themes of this rhetoric—monopoly, feudalism, loss of opportunity and democracy—were constant refrains of the anti-chain movement's leading lights. Representative Wright Patman (D-Texas), one of the most prominent small-business advocates in Congress, put it this way: "The wide distribution of economic power among many independent proprietors is the foundation of the Nation's economy. Both Franklin and Jefferson feared that industrialization would lead to a labor proletariat without property and without hope. Small-business enterprise is a symbol of a society where a hired man can become his own boss. . . . History shows that the elimination of the independent businessman has been the first step in the development of totalitarianism."[9]

The concrete expression of such political rhetoric was the anti–chain store law enacted in individual states. At the federal level, bills were introduced to enact laws hostile to chains, but these never gained sufficient support. The most prominent example was the bill—eventually defeated—introduced in 1938 by Patman with seventy-five cosponsors. That bill, called a "death sentence" by chain entrepreneurs, would have effectively outlawed large national chains, most of which would have been levied with tax bills that exceeded their total earnings.

The idea of state legislation against chains was first introduced at the 1922 convention of the National Association of Retail Grocers, where the desirability of restricting the number of chain stores in any one community was discussed. The following year, a law of that type was introduced in Missouri but did not pass. In 1927, Maryland enacted a law that disallowed any chain that operated more than five stores in Allegany County. The law was judged unconstitutional by the circuit court of Allegany County, mainly because the distinction between more and less than five stores was arbitrary. Similar laws in North Carolina and Georgia received similar judgments from the state Supreme Courts. Laws passed in 1929 in Indiana and North Carolina represented a significant variation, in that they applied increasing taxes to chains starting with the second rather than the fifth store. A 1931 ruling by the U.S. Supreme Court upheld the Indiana law. The key element of the majority opinion was that the distinction between single-unit and multi-unit organizations was neither arbitrary nor unreasonable, with the astounding growth of chains cited as proof that there were differences and advantages in their favor. This ruling opened a floodgate of anti-chain legislation, which had been pent up by past negative rulings at the state level. As one observer put it, "wherever a little band of lawmakers are gathered together in the sacred name of legislation, you can be sure that they are thinking up things they can do to the chain stores."[10] In the years that followed, hundreds of anti-chain bills were introduced at the state level. Dozens passed, and ultimately twenty-seven of the forty-eight states enacted anti-chain laws in the interwar period.

The pro-chain forces formed organizations to manage their collective action and converted existing organizations to their purpose. Among the most significant was the National Chain Store Association (NCSA), created in 1928 through the merger of two regional associations in the grocery industry. The NCSA's efforts included the publication of 400,000 copies of a monthly bulletin, as well as the publication and distribution of several hundred thousand pamphlets and editorial reprints and a debaters' manual. Much of the content of these publications was created by the NCSA's own research bureau, headed by Paul C. Olsen of Columbia University. The NCSA also maintained a legal defense fund ($175,000 in each of 1933 and 1934) for battling state anti-chain laws. In 1933 the president of A&P, then the largest chain in the land, threatened closure, but three years later waged an expensive and extensive battle against the anti-chain laws. A&P alone bought space in 1,300 newspapers and sent its spokesmen out to address thousands of civic organizations.

The anti-chain forces thrived in the court of public opinion, and their numbers, and the organization of their interests, drove the passing of anti-chain laws. The pro-chain forces were ineffectual in that context, but their relative wealth and centralization and their strategy of legally contesting anti-chain laws gained influence in the judicial arena. Decisions by the U.S. Supreme Court, both for and against anti-chain laws, thus exerted effects on the repeal of such laws by legislatures. The pro-chain forces hired a leading advertising agency, Lord & Thomas, to manage their public relations campaign, which had two legs: the recognition that they had made mistakes during their rapid growth coupled with an onslaught of radio commercials and newspaper advertising. According to polls conducted by *Fortune* magazine in 1937, slightly more than half of interviewees favored a special tax on chains. By 1939, only 37.5 percent supported such a tax.[11] The high point of anti-chain legislation came in 1937, after which the repeal and lapse of existing laws outweighed the passage of new ones.

■ The Spread of Chain Store Taxes

The owners of independent businesses and chains represented the opposing sides: independent entrepreneurs were consistently for anti-chain laws, while chain entrepreneurs were consistently against them. The greater the number of independent stores in a state, the more influential they were with legislators and the more likely the state was to enact laws specifying punitive taxes on chain stores. For example, one U.S. senator explained his anti-chain position as a function of the "hundreds of letters [received] from individual merchants for every one that comes from a chain store official or employee."[12] Conversely, chains became more consequential for legislators as they became more numerous and were thus able to prevent the enactment of anti–chain store laws.

Although the number of constituents with a given interest and their resources may be the raw material of power, the organization harnesses that power. In turn, the capacity to organize effectively hinges on whether constituents recognize their shared identity and by implication their shared interests.[13] The ability of independent stores to organize an effective anti–chain store campaign was hindered by the fact that druggists, cigar store owners, and grocery store owners all needed to band together. Given the ethnic segmentation of retailing throughout most of this century (e.g., the dominance of Jewish owners in dry goods retailing), this may have frustrated organization in heterogeneous retail sectors.

By contrast, since there were fewer chains, they were able to develop a shared identity and became a centralized interest group. For instance, the California State Chain Store Association was made up of only sixty-five chains, and they shared the costs of the campaign according to their size; some chains, such as Safeway Groceries, which faced an annual tax of $669,011, were willing to bear almost all of the costs of contention, allowing others such as the Regal Shoe Company ($7 in annual taxes) to free-ride.

For the independents, however, there were no giants to lead the group, and eliciting contributions required making thousands of individual sales pitches. Still, the influence of heterogeneity in frustrating independent organization appears to be one of degree—there were some instances, such as the various trade-at-home campaigns, where independents achieved some degree of coordination and organization. Such collective action was more likely to occur when the independents in a state belonged to the same retail segment and had a shared identity (e.g., the department store segment, which is large, has many independents). When independent stores were concentrated in one segment, it was easier to crystallize a shared identity and spark collective organization. Independent concentration in a segment in a state had a dramatic effect on the rate of enactment of chain store tax laws.

Pro–chain store forces prevented the enactment of anti–chain store laws when they were numerous and influential. Moreover, their efforts to derail anti-chain tax laws were helped by organized labor's openness to chain stores. In 1938 and 1939 the largest chain in the country, A&P, which had previously resisted unionization, signed a series of collective bargaining contracts with AFL unions under the guidance of their public relations counsel in a bid to repair the image of chains. The value of these contracts was demonstrated in 1940 when Wright Patman's federal "Death Sentence Bill"—which nearly outlawed chains by taxing them to bankruptcy—was vigorously opposed by the International Allied Printing Trades Association, the International Retail Clerks' Protective Association, the Amalgamated Meat Cutters and Butcher Workmen (all AFL affiliates), and by numerous union locals and state federations of labor.

Moreover, jobs in chains paid better: in 1933 the average chain employee earned $1,079 per year, compared to $945 for independent employees. Even workers in the lowest levels of a chain hierarchy had at least the possibility of promotion to a better position, unlike workers in independent organizations, who were always subordinate to the owner-operator. Thus employees in independently owned stores became a constituency that supported chain stores and thwarted anti–chain store laws. The number of employees in independently owned stores substantially depressed the rate of enactment of chain store tax laws.[14]

Contention in states spilled into other states, and tactics of contention diffused. For example, in 1936 the *New York Times* mentioned anti-chain contestation in California in seven different articles. Iowa came in second with four articles, mostly as a result of its particularly large tax—an outcome of the strength of the anti-chain forces in Iowa. Pro-chain tactics such as forming a state association, and anti-chain tactics such as the march on the state capital, would have had a chance to influence contention in other states before the outcome in California was even known. As evidence of this effect, California's anti-chain contention was discussed at a meeting of retail grocers in Dallas in June 1936, five months before the referendum. Whether a state becomes an influential role model for anti-chain outcomes or pro-chain outcomes hinges on the strength of the contending forces. States where the revenues of independently owned stores were large became influential role models for the enactment of anti–chain store laws in other states. By contrast, states with large chain store revenues were significant role models for opposition to such laws and impeded their promulgation in other states.[15]

■ The Rollback of Chain Store Taxes

In states with anti–chain store laws, pro–chain store forces were able to roll back the laws because of support from an unlikely source: farmers. Farmers were initially viewed as unsympathetic to the urban, northeastern, capitalistic values that the chains represented. Chains also represented a direct threat to the economic interests of rural America by consolidating purchasing power in the retail food industry. It has always been recognized that one of the economic advantages of chains was purchasing power wrought by consolidation. But such power came at the expense of sellers, and in the service industry where chains had the most sales, food retailing, those sellers were farmers.

Bumper crops that created surpluses and gluts brought farmers and chains together. A striking example was the California referendum campaign of 1936 to rescind the anti–chain store tax. Early in the year, growers and canners were threatened by a peach surplus. On February 26, the California Canning Peach Growers wrote to Don Francisco, the Lord & Thomas vice president who "quarterbacked" the chains' referendum campaign, explaining the crisis and attributing it to an underconsumption of canned peaches. Francisco played the broker in this instance, and through their national association, the chains launched a nationwide drive to purchase and distribute the peaches. The growers realized a substantial gain, rather than the loss they feared. Similar efforts occurred to help California cattlemen and the dried fruit industry. Following the California experience, the grocery chains instituted a permanent agricultural relief program, which in subsequent years moved many surplus crops into consumption across the nation. In Florida in 1937, A&P stepped in to save the citrus industry from a surplus just as the state senate was about to pass a particularly harsh antichain bill. Citrus growers spoke up, and the bill was defeated. In that year in Maine, the pressure of farm groups caused the repeal of a chain tax. Farm groups also spoke against antichain laws in Oregon (walnut growers) and New York (turkey farmers).

These examples involved coordination between chains and agricultural cooperatives rather than disorganized farmers. Key individuals brokered the connection between chains and cooperatives. John Brandt, president of the massive Land O' Lakes dairy cooperative, was a featured speaker at the second annual meeting of the NCSA. He attributed the rapid growth of his organization to the chains that bought 75 percent of its output.[16] James E. Boyle, an agricultural economist at Cornell, proselytized the chain–co-op connection at meetings of both camps. NCSA executives such as vice president R. W. Lyons advised farmers that working with chains would "require grower organization, agreement to furnish quality in exactly the kind of uniform packs demanded by chain store business.... Some individuals of course can comply with these requirements but these are among the larger growers. Smaller ones must pool their efforts."[17]

The link between chains and agricultural co-ops is unusual because cooperatives are seen as representatives of an economic order that challenges corporations. So how did agricultural cooperatives and chains resolve this incongruence? Fantastically, a claim took hold that they were fundamentally the same type of organization. Brandt of Land O'Lakes characterized agricultural cooperatives as an instance of "the chain idea of production and merchandising."[18] The general manager of a cooperative of California date growers observed that "the chains represent organized, efficient mass distribution, which is the counterpart of organized selling by a farmer cooperative."[19] Agricultural cooperatives started to embrace concepts of efficiency and rationality. At the time of the anti-chain episode, both the distribution and agricultural sectors were lagging in the rationalization that was coming to define the modern American economy. Co-ops and chains represented the vanguard of rationalization in their respective sectors, the first organizational forms in those sectors to successfully apply managerial control and coordination. They occupied very similar market positions—chains accounted for 22 percent of retail sales in 1929, while co-ops accounted for 23 percent of agricultural sales in 1930. Agricultural cooperatives did not face direct competition from corporations—corporate farms (and other larger-than-family farms) did not begin to flourish until after World War II.

Whatever the rhetorical underpinnings of the chain–co-op brokerage, the historical record suggests that co-ops helped the chains.[20] For example, during the momentous California referendum of 1936, the managers of peach, avocado, citrus, olive, dairy, and date cooperatives gave testimonials in favor of the chains, while no independent farms, which were at that time the large majority in California agriculture, appeared in the pro-chain propaganda.[21] Co-op leaders were similarly vocal in opposition to the Patman "death-sentence" bill in hearings before a subcommittee of the U.S. House of Representatives. Cooperatives had a significant impact on the ability of pro-chain forces to induce the repeal of chain store tax laws.

The simultaneous examination of the anti–chain store movement and the pro–chain store interest group highlights their interdependence. At the most basic level, the parties animated each other—the anti-chain movement began as a response to a rapid proliferation of chains; leaders of chain organizations shifted from explicit disregard to intense engagement of the anti-chain movement in response to its early successes. Pro-chain forces were losing out in states and appealed to a higher power (the Supreme Court) to review the constitutionality of anti-chain laws. This maneuvering may be seen as an instance of the general tendency of disadvantaged groups to strive to make conflict more "public" and widen it, whereas the advantaged seek to make it "private" and limit it.[22]

The independents, disadvantaged vis-à-vis the chain stores in terms of resources and organization, chose the most public forums, the grassroots of public opinion and the legislatures. In contrast, the chain stores exploited their advantage in the rarified and exclusive environs of the courts. Contention in this latter forum was further circumscribed by the legal strategies of the chains, which emphasized the cultural, constitutive element of the law.[23] They focused on erudite questions regarding the boundaries of organizational forms (e.g., how many units define a chain?) and the legitimate bases for inter-form comparisons (e.g., how is a chain different from a department store?), rather than the materialistic issues of wealth distribution and organizational survival that were more appealing to the public.

The greater the number of Supreme Court decisions that annulled anti–chain store laws, the easier it was for pro-chain forces to annul anti-chain laws in a focal state. Judicial precedents became institutions that curtailed the discretion of legislatures.[24] As the number of Supreme Court decisions striking down such laws rose, the rate of repeal of chain store tax laws increased enormously.

■ **Implications**

It was not only the number of independent stores but their homogeneity and the influence of role models that drove the enactment of anti-chain laws. This seems to map onto the grassroots social movement activity at the state level, which represented the main effort of the anti-chain camp. When chains and their allies—the independent employees—were more numerous, anti-chain tax laws were less likely to be passed.

By contrast, repeals of anti-chain legislation were largely shaped by the existence of cooperatives and negative Supreme Court decisions. Decisions against anti-chain laws led directly to repeal, while positive decisions discouraged diffusion of repeal from state to state. The contest over repeal, it would seem, was played on the turf of the chains. They had national interests, national organization, and a national strategy of fighting in the courts. The independents, on the other hand, were local in every sense and their success hinged on overcoming diversity with a cohesive identity. The key to the ultimate success of the chains was their success in shifting the arena of contention from the local level and the grassroots to the national level and the Supreme Court.

Independent stores could not compete with chains on the basis of economic efficiency; instead, they resorted to "non-market" strategies. Their choice was to organize and pressure legislators to enact laws hostile to chains; laws were not an "external" variable affecting organization. On the one side, it was the organization of independents that affected the rate of enactment of chain store tax laws. These laws protected independent stores and preserved their markets by imposing punitive penalties on chain stores. On the other side, it was the political influence of chain forces that significantly affected the repeal of anti-chain laws. The saga of the anti–chain store episode shows that social movements and interest groups within an industry struggle at the boundaries of an organizational form (in our case, chains). The issue is not whether the boundaries of a form such as chain stores are efficient but whether they are socially and politically acceptable. Organizational forms and their boundaries are institutional settlements rather than just the outcome of efficiency.

When independents belonged to one retail segment, they were able to develop a shared identity, to mobilize more easily and pressure legislators to enact anti–chain store laws, and to prevent their repeal. Rival arguments exist as to which group, chains or independents, more closely reflected Americans' core values. There can be no doubt, however, as to which group was better positioned to generate a cohesive identity and to organize around it. Chain entrepreneurs were few in number, geographically concentrated, and shared a status as challengers to the established economic order. Independent retailers were as diverse as the American population (and almost as numerous). Of course, the latter group struggled to cohere, mobilize, and organize. It is not that they were unable to act—they presented an impressive array of contentious actions, ranging from radio broadcasts to inflammatory cartoons to high school debates. But these actions were insufficiently focused and coordinated to overcome the chains' effort. Our results also reveal that the existence of allies significantly affected the likelihood of the enactment of anti-chain laws and their repeal. Chain stores relied on brokers to co-opt potential adversaries. The brokers, hired public relations professionals, counseled and mediated for the chains to transform their relationships with farmers and workers.

The anti–chain store episode, with its emphasis on local identities, resonates with the ongoing movement to thwart the expansion by Wal-Mart and other big box retailers by communities concerned about small business, sprawl, and congestion. If anti–chain store opponents in the 1920s used tax laws to thwart chains, their modern-day counterparts rely on zoning regulations to check the chains' advance. If anti–chain store opponents in the 1920s framed chain stores as a threat to local businesses and the local communities, their modern counterparts also connect chain stores to urban sprawl and the destruction of small-town cultures and businesses. The movement against superstores has brought together conservationists, community activists, and small business owners, all of whom have rallied around the slogan "Sprawl or Community."

A global echo of the movement against chain stores is the worldwide Slow Food movement, begun in 1986 to oppose the fast food sold by chains. When McDonald's opened a franchise near the Spanish Steps in Rome, Carlo Petrini, a leader of the gastronomical branch of ARCI, used a cool technique of mobilization to protest—a pasta-eating contest in which first prize was awarded to the slowest eater. Petrini and his followers proclaimed that Rome was about "slow food," not "fast food," and celebrated local and seasonal cuisine.

The success of the demonstration and the organizational infrastructure of the Communist-affiliated ARCI led to the emergence of the Slow Food movement in Italy. The dissident Communist newspaper *Il Manifesto* originally published the gastronomical supplement called *Gambero Rosso* (the Red Crab), which later grew into the Slow Food movement's authoritative restaurant and wine guides. The Slow Food movement sought to rediscover regional tastes and cuisines. Its symbol was the snail, and it sought to protest

"McDomination." Its motto was "A firm defense of quiet material pleasure is the only way to oppose the universal folly of Fast Life."

Local units called *convivia* were created and they relied on volunteers—the founders of the *convivia* were mostly gastronomic experts, journalists who published in food and wine magazines, and restaurateurs. The spread of the *convivia* and *Gambero Rosso* meant the rebirth of *osteria*— traditional Italian inns that preserved old methods and techniques of cooking. Soon, the Slow Food movement's evangelists realized that the concept of slowness had to be applied not only to the consumption but also to the production of food, and promoted organic methods of agriculture that would produce "good" food. In 1996, Slow Food started the Ark of Taste project to preserve distinctive animal breeds, cheeses, meats, fruits, grains, and herbs whose existence was threatened by the "supermarket culture." Such foods included the purple asparagus of Albenga, the black celery of Trevi, the Vesuvian apricot, the long-tailed sheep of Laticauda, and a succulent Sienese pig renowned in the courts of medieval Tuscany. To support the Ark Project, the movement created *presidia*, or defense battalions, entrusted with the task of saving and renewing prized species such as the Piedmontese cow. Restaurants were also encouraged to include an endangered product in their menu. Thus, the Slow Food movement became an eco-gastronomic movement; it defended small producers and sought to encourage cooking.

By 1999 Slow Food had grown rather quickly to a membership of more than 70,000, with supporters in thirty-five countries. Its diffusion into other countries meant very different kinds of protest. In contrast to the sit-in organized by Petrini and his followers in the Piazza Spagna, Jose Bove, the French activist turned farmer, drove a tractor into a McDonald's in Millau in southern France. He and his associates left graffiti—"Mac Go Home" and "Guardians of Roquefort." They sought to protest a 100 percent tax increase on French Roquefort cheese by the United States in response to a French increase of tariffs on hormone-treated American beef. Bove defined his move as an attack on McDomination and on junk food: "'For us . . . McDonald's is a symbol of a multinational who wants everybody in the world to eat the same way. It's a symbol of industrial agriculture.'"[25] By 2004 Slow Food had 80,000 members in more than 100 countries, organized into almost 800 local *convivia*, and had sponsored the University of Gastronomic Sciences in Italy.

The anti–chain store movement, the movement against big box stores, and the movement against fast food all signal that the expansion of a dominant organizational form triggers competition from other weaker organizational forms. The latter rely on a "non-market" strategy to take on their superior competitor and defend not just their position but their very identity, and this takes the form of grassroots mobilization and either the enactment of new laws, the enforcement of existing laws, or the ratcheting of public pressure to contain the expansion of the predatory organizational form. Chains, super stores, and McDonald's respond to non-market initiatives with non-market counterstrikes of their own, be it lobbying trade associations to repeal laws, mass advertising campaigns, or pro-social behaviors such as social responsibility campaigns.

The non-market strategies deployed by rebels seeking to protect local identities of small towns are in the "streets." But how do they get into "suites" to shape the decision-making of top managers of large firms? In chapter 7, I turn to this issue but analyze it in the context of market rebels seeking to prevent the introduction of a new technology—in this instance, biotechnology—into the German market. I show how the anti-biotechnology movement penetrated their targets—large German pharmaceutical firms—and prevented them from commercializing their knowledge.

Drug Wars
How the Anti-Biotechnology Movement Penetrated German Pharmaceutical Firms and Prevented Technology Commercialization

Germany was one of the very first nations to commit to biotechnology research in the postwar era. By 1972, the Federal Research Ministry, under the aegis of the Social Democrats, developed a biotechnology development plan that established a national laboratory to promote biotechnology research.[1] By 1981, the Federal Research Ministry concluded that the plan neglected genetic engineering, and decided to change its focus. The ministry built three institutes in Munich, Heidelberg, and Cologne to focus on genetic engineering. In 1982, the new Christian Democratic Union–led government augmented support for biotechnology even further and doubled subsidies by 1988 to DM 261 million. Per capita, Germans applied for more biotechnology patents than did Americans.[2] Things were looking good for German biotech.

But by 1990 German pharmaceutical firms either had plants sitting idle, like Heochst AG's $37 million facility in Frankfurt, or had delayed construction on new plants, like Bayer's plants to manufacture genetically engineered protein for hemophiliacs. While plants and plans idled, 75 percent of German biotechnology investments flowed past German borders, especially to the United States. BASF established a lab in Worcester, Massachusetts, Bayer targeted Berkeley,

California, and Henkel based its operations in Santa Rosa, California.[3] And by 2000, 61 percent of Germans disagreed with the statement that biotechnology would benefit them—only Spain and France had even worse public attitudes toward biotechnology.[4] Moreover, while large pharmaceutical firms had accumulated many biotechnology patents, there were no German biotechnology start-up firms. These only appeared on the landscape in 1995 after a venture capital industry arose in Germany.

What happened? Why were German firms unable to produce biotech products in Germany? Why were they unable to commercialize the knowledge they already had? Why did they have to relocate their laboratories in the United States? Why could they not transfer knowledge from their laboratories in the United States to Germany? In this chapter I draw on an intensive study of six large German pharmaceutical firms to demonstrate how they were penetrated by market rebels spearheading the anti-biotechnology movement.

The anti-biotechnology movement was not a mass movement with strikes or marches. Public opposition to biotechnology was fueled by an anti-biotechnology movement of about sixty disparate groups that were opposed to different aspects of biotechnology. The groups ranged from Christian activists to the Rote Zora (or Red Cells)—an eco-feminist group; in the middle were groups like Citizens Watching Petunias. It was this diverse set of rebels that impeded German pharmaceutical firms. How and why did these powerful pharmaceutical firms succumb to a motley band of market rebels?

The answer to this puzzle lies in how the strength of the

anti-biotechnology movement interacted with the internal processes of the pharmaceutical firms.[5] The strength of the anti-biotechnology movement stemmed from how its adherents framed their message, from their unconventional tactics and networks of mobilization, and from the political opportunity they enjoyed because of their ties to the Green Party. In regions where the anti-biotechnology movement was strong, it was able to undermine the legitimacy of biotechnology by arousing anxiety about the risks and enacting restrictive regional laws that increased uncertainty for firms. Such regulatory uncertainty undermined the champions of biotechnology projects in German firms, who had to overcome skepticism from the chemical engineers who dominated the executive boards of large, public German pharmaceutical firms. Regulatory uncertainty made biotechnology risky and undercut the underlying investment models, and executive boards voted instead to allocate resources to safer chemical projects.

The anti-biotechnology movement also attacked the identities of scientists working on biotechnology projects. Large, public German pharmaceutical firms located R&D laboratories specializing in biotechnology overseas in the United States, but they were unable to exploit their knowledge because scientists who had been transferred from overseas labs to Germany were reluctant to work on biotech projects. By contrast, small, private German firms were immune from these pressures because they were located in areas where the anti-biotechnology movement was weak, and thus did not face legitimacy threats. Since they were private, they could think of the long term and exploit their knowledge.

■ The Commercial Biotechnology Sector in Germany, 1980–95

In contrast to the United States, where small biotech start-ups staffed by university professors and financed by venture capitalists commercialized biotechnology, in Germany large pharmaceutical firms were the prime actors during the 1980s and mid-1990s. Small biotechnology firms financed by venture capitalists appeared on the landscape much later. Thus German pharmaceutical firms had to bear the brunt of the opposition to recombinant technologies that was sparked by environmentalists, feminists, religious fundamentalists, and Green Party members, all of whom constituted the core of the anti-biotech movement.

Genetic engineering, while originally peripheral to the Greens, became salient when pharmaceutical companies started moving into large-scale biotechnological production processes in the mid-1980s. The Green Party widened its environmental position beyond the traditional issues of nuclear energy and chemical pollution. Church groups opposed to the manipulation of life hardened their views, which were shaped by the debate over abortion during the mid- to late 1970s. Feminist groups were vociferous in their opposition to genetic engineering: the Rote Zora carried out a series of nine arson attacks on genetic research institutes and companies between 1984 and 1989.

Activism in the biomedical domain peaked between 1984 and 1991. The resonance of genetic engineering as a "lightning rod issue" ebbed after the promulgation of a federal law in 1990 that stringently regulated facilities in which biotechnological processes were used. The law was revised in 1992 and endorsed by a broad parliamentary majority; this revision relaxed the early restrictions. The mid-1990s saw the surge of biotech start-ups in Germany, triggered by government support and a nascent venture capital industry. By the late 1990s, some German pharmaceutical firms had arguably fallen behind in utilizing the new technology while others were more successful in moving forward.

The anti-biotechnology movement was powered by a motley band of a hundred or so radical activists. Prominent among them were Ulrike Riedel, who had been a nuclear energy activist, became the secretary of Joschka Fischer (minister for energy and the environment), and was a Green Party member; Regine Kollek, a biologist at the Ökoinstitut Freiburg who had studied genetic engineering in the United States; and Jens Katzek, an activist in BUND (a moderate environmental organization in Germany). Other groups, such as the GENEthische Netzwerk (GID), and militants with ties to feminist and anarchist groups, such as the Rote Zora, also were active. How could such a small, diverse, and initially peripheral group of radicals mobilize the larger public for its cause and have an impact?

Of the top six biotech firms, Schering AG, Boehringer Ingelheim (BI), and Boehringer Mannheim (BM) were successful in launching new products during the 1990s, while Bayer, Hoechst, and BASF were laggards. Ironically, Hoechst and Bayer were early movers with recombinant insulin in 1982 (even if Bayer never sold much), but they could not translate that early advantage into a stream of new and original products in the 1990s. Hoechst started a high-profile co-operation with Massachusetts General Hospital in 1981, which included the training of Hoechst's R&D scientists there, and Bayer forged an alliance in 1982–83 with Genentech in the area of hematology and set up research facilities in New Haven and later Berkeley. BM and BI were early movers as well, but they were able to commercialize new products during and after the main opposition years. Schering was a late entrant and together with BI and BM was the only German pharmaceutical company to discover and develop its own biotechnology products. BASF was the company with the smallest pharmaceutical business unit of the six and was unsuccessful. Why did Hoechst and Bayer lag behind the others despite their early successes? And why were the two Boehringer companies and Schering able to be more effective in their commercialization efforts despite movement opposition to the technology? I draw on one detailed study of the German pharmaceutical industry to address this issue.[6]

■ Making the Dangers of Biotechnology into a Hot Cause

New technologies can only thrive when they possess legitimacy—when they are unquestioned by consumers, financiers, employees, and governmental authorities. The small, diverse band of anti-biotechnology activists were able to frame genetic engineering as dangerous and risky, to exploit unconventional tactics of mobilization, and to harness their connections with the Green Party to push through legislation that stifled technology commercialization.

The Rise of the Green Party

Within three years of its founding, the Green Party was in the national parliament (Bundestag) and then in virtually all state assemblies. Representation in the national parliament allowed the Greens to be part of the Enquete Komission described below. Yet regional representation at the city and state levels was equally decisive because approval and monitoring of industrial facilities that were regulated by federal or state law were delegated to the state level and to regional administrative units within states that were headed by political appointees of the state government (Regierungspräsidien). In addition, city governments could implement zoning laws and building restrictions. The Green Party gained access to state parliaments in rapid succession during the 1980s: Baden-Württemberg (location of BI and BM) in 1980, Berlin (Schering) in 1981, Hesse (Hoechst) in 1982, Bavaria (BM) in 1986, Rhineland-Palatine (BASF) in 1987, and Northrhine-Westphalia (Bayer) in 1990.

The Greens had political power in only one state, Hesse, because they were part of the coalition of government. All other states were ruled by Christian Democrats or Social Democrats. Hoechst's location in Hesse put it at a disadvantage. In late 1984, Hoechst applied for a permit under the existing emission control law (Immissionsschutzgesetz) to operate a facility for producing recombinant insulin near Frankfurt. The facility was approved by the regional Regierungspräsidium in June 1985, based on a recommendation of the ZKBS, a national panel of scientists for the voluntary safety assessment and self-regulation of biotechnological facilities. In

December 1985, the Green Party entered into a coalition government with the Social Democratic Party (SPD) in Hesse, and Joschka Fischer became minister for energy and the environment. Soon, Hoechst's bid for a permit for the second stage of the insulin facility was rejected. It submitted an amended application, and a new permit was granted in May 1986, only to be revoked, and then approved by the pro-business CDU-FDP government that emerged from state elections in April. At this stage, Green activists filed suits and tied up Hoechst in court. By contrast, BI had applied for the operation of its general purpose biofermentation plant in Biberach the same year as Hoechst. The approval was granted within three months thanks to the pro-business CDU head of the state government, Lothar Späth.

Paradoxically, then, the anti-biotechnology movement was strongest in terms of access to political support and mobilizing potential in the very states where the large, publicly traded German pharmaceutical firms were located, and weak in states where smaller private firms were located.

Depicting Biotechnology as Nazi Eugenics

The success of a protest movement hinges on how activists frame their target or enemy, and in particular how they make claims that are connected to resonant cultural narratives and everyday experiences of their audience.[7] German anti-biotech activists attacked biotechnology by depicting it as a Faustian bargain with the devil that risked resurrecting Nazi eugenics and genetic discrimination. They also relied on dramatic gestures that aroused the emotions of their audience, and their opponents—the pharmaceutical firms—were left reeling because they relied on a strategy of presenting "facts." The result was that activists were able to portray the actions of their targets—German pharmaceutical firms—as dangerous, unsafe, immoral, and illegitimate.

German activists depicted biotechnology as a man-made technology that meddles with nature to produce "Frankensteins." In one public debate, the moral theologian Franz Boeckle argued that experiments for manipulating the human germline should be denied on principle and without exception. Anti-biotechnology activists also exploited a deep-seated German taboo against genetic discrimination. Genetic engineering was portrayed as Nazi eugenics and therefore dangerous to society, whereas opposition to genetic engineering was equated with dignity for the individual and for community. A 1985 pamphlet of the radical Genetischen Informationsdienst (GID) pointed out that some genetic researchers studied under proponents of eugenics during the Nazi regime and were apologists of "social hygiene."

Such emotionally resonant framings enabled the small group of core activists to broaden their appeal to recruit a wide range of allies and sympathizers such as workers within pharmaceutical companies, schoolteachers, neighbors of scientists, church groups and leaders, politicians across the political spectrum, and part of the scientific community. In turn, these groups created their own organizations. For instance, support from the Ökoinstitut, an independent, environmentally oriented think tank created in 1977 by respected scientists opposed to nuclear energy, gave scientific credibility to arguments against biotechnology. By reducing biotechnology to genetic engineering and connecting it to Nazi eugenics, the anti-biotech activists made biotechnology a matter of basic principles and a technology imbued with "incalculable risk," a term borrowed from the parallel debate about nuclear energy. As a result, defenders were hard-pressed to justify the safety of specific projects. As early as 1984–85, a parliamentary Enquete Komission (a multiparty ad hoc commission that focused on key societal issues) was entrusted with writing a report on biotechnology and titled it "Opportunities and Risks of Genetic Technology." By contrast, the Office of Technology Assessment in the United States had released a report titled "Commercial Biotechnology," which reviewed the economic prospects of the technology and how the federal government could support the industry. Anti-biotechnology activists aroused public anxiety about the "incalculable risks" of biotechnology around "emission control" (Freisetzung)—a framing also borrowed from the nuclear energy debate. E-coli bacteria that were altered to produce insulin were presented as sources of "incalculable risk" if they ever entered the natural world.

If Green activists made the emission of transgenic organisms into an unspoiled nature as a hazard, religious conservatives and the women's movement were inflamed in 1988 when the Christian Democrat–led German government endorsed the European Human Genome project, which included a "predictive medicine" program focused on prenatal genetic screening techniques. Religious conservatives inveighed against it as "a European abortion program motivated by eugenics," and women's groups attacked genetic counseling as "continuations of Nazi eugenics." This controversy was fueled by the infamous "Singer Affair." Peter Singer, a controversial Australian bioethicist, had coauthored with Helga Kuse a book titled *Should the Baby Live?* (1993), arguing that it was ethical to abort fetuses with severe disabilities because they lacked the human capacity to experience agony and determine their own fate. When Singer was lecturing at a bioethics conference, he drew jeers and catcalls. Oliver Tolmein, a lawyer, journalist, self-described "anti-bioethicist," and leader of the "Cripples Movement," wrote that debating with Singer was "as senseless as debating a theory arguing for the superiority of the Aryan race." As a consequence of such events, public anxiety about biotechnology increased and broadened into an ever wider set of concerns. One observer nicely summarized the strategy of the anti-biotechnology activists, saying, "The problem also should be diffuse, not concrete, look threatening and dangerous, almost mysterious, a mystical global angst, look at the Frankenstein images, lots of blood and deformations, etc. in activist stunts. And if you get that mix, you're almost unbeatable, this is exactly the propaganda principle of dictators like the Nazis and Stalinists, very effective and smart."[8]

■ **Cool Mobilization through Smart and Beautiful Tactics**

Anti-biotechnology activists relied on public street protests and marches not only to gain media attention but also to mobilize the public. Often they were local exercises, lacking mass character and national scale. For example, activists protesting a planned facility for producing recombinant

Figure 7.1
Protesting patents on life in Germany.
V.Listl/argum/Greenpeace.

EPO (erythropoietin) in the town of Marburg in 1989 staged
a traditional street march of about six hundred people, while
a Greenpeace group peacefully blocked the access road to the
Bayer headquarters through a sit-down protest, a format
widely used in 1960s student protests and opposition to U.S.
missile facilities in the early 1980s. Figure 7.1 shows a group of
activists protesting the award of biotechnology patents and
gaining media coverage.

In some neighborhoods near pharmaceutical compa-
nies, activists distributed leaflets to employees and residents,
a practice that had been successfully used by environmentalist groups protesting water and air pollution. From 1982 onward, activists took advantage of a law that gave every shareholder the right to ask questions and speak at the annual

meeting (AGM) of a particular company. Ten to fifty activists would each buy a single share in a company like Bayer or Hoechst and use the AGM to voice their opinions, force a vote on the resignation of the management, and press environmental demands. News coverage and the public embarrassment of the company's management heightened the effectiveness of this tactic. Opponents would use provisions in building and environmental regulations to demand public hearings when new facilities were being planned and file objections that needed to be addressed by the permit applicant before the approval process could be continued. In several cases—for example, at Hoechst, Grünenthal, and Behringwerke—activists distributed ready-made forms that local residents only had to sign and file. Finally, some core activists resorted to exhausting legal means, suing companies in court for violating emission-control legislation and procedural violations. The ability of activists to pressure specific companies varied regionally, and also depended on companies' salience and accessibility.

The cities of Frankfurt, Cologne, and Berlin in particular had large and well-connected activist communities centered around left-leaning universities that had played a key role in the student protests of the 1960s, in the emerging Green Party, and around left-wing union organizers. The Frankfurt area, for example, had seen some of the earliest and most confrontational environmentalist protests in the late 1970s around nearby nuclear power plants and the airport extension. By contrast, in most rural areas, and in some cities like Munich, early opponents of biotechnology lacked access and critical mass, and local activists lacked experience.

Additionally, potential targets varied in their accessibility. A company's size, ownership structure, and history further affect its saliency and accessibility. For example, privately held pharmaceutical companies do not hold annual general meetings, eliminating one access point available in the case of public companies. Family-owned businesses are more secretive about their activities and thus receive less coverage in the media. Large companies serve as exemplars for the industry and are highly visible in the news, while smaller companies are more likely to operate under the radar. Companies with a history of environmental violations are already monitored by vigilant activists.

In terms of regional exposure to the movement, the operations of Hoechst, Bayer, BASF, and Schering were located in left-leaning cities; BM and BI located their biotechnology activities in conservative rural areas. Hoechst, Bayer, BASF, and Schering were publicly traded, while BM and BI were family owned. Hoechst, Bayer, and BASF were large companies with chemicals business units that already were targeted by environmentalists, while the others were smaller pharmaceutical specialists. Hoechst, Bayer, BASF, BI, and BM sought to build recombinant production facilities between 1984 and 1989. Unsurprisingly, when the factors of location, size, ownership, business scope, and plans for large-scale production plants are combined, Hoechst, Bayer, and BASF were more strongly pressured by opponents to genetic engineering than were BM and BI. Schering, although publicly traded and located in Berlin, never sought to enter large-scale biotechnological production in Germany.

Anti-biotechnology activists benefited from a mass

media already primed to cover environmental issues as a result of the novelty of the Green Party, and from norms of balanced reporting in the public broadcasting system in Germany. Personal contacts between activists and critical and investigative reporters from shared experiences in leftist student groups also provided ready access.

Activists gained and sustained media exposure through skillful tactics. To arouse public concern, they held protests at large physical structures, such as corporate fermentation plants, rather than small university laboratories. As one activist put it,

> It is hard to get people to do something about invisible microbes in garden soil or unspectacular university labs, where do you go to protest? This is not like nuclear power plants where you have a locale. So initially we had to turn to commercial companies because they were more concrete targets . . . so the protests were about insulin fermentation and the first field experiments with recombinant petunias . . . both more technical issues, less about some of the real ethical questions that we were concerned about, and not that well supported by scientific arguments either. Companies for that reason probably sometimes got a harsher treatment than they deserved, but in the larger scheme of things that was necessary to push the issue.[9]

Concrete and strong enemies, such as pharmaceutical companies or research laboratories in universities, were psychologically salient targets of negative attention that enabled activists to dramatize a system's inherent contradictions and vulnerabilities. Activists staged dramatic spectacles to garner TV coverage and make the dangers of biotechnology more vivid: headless chickens strutting before demonstrations, disabled protestors holding signs against reproductive genetic screening, deformed mutant mice in animal testing cages. While necessary for reaching a broader public, the expediency and vividness of corporate facilities as targets also narrowed and directed the scope of issues discussed in public—for example, a predominant focus on emission safety at the expense of more general ethical issues. The activist's increased mobilizing capacity came at the price of a decreased range of protest issues.

Anti-biotech activists used existing legitimate forums and arenas of media attention to their advantage by placing great emphasis on local podium discussions, talk shows, parliamentary debates, and scientific institutes. For example, the Enquete Komission enabled Green activists and parliamentarians to take part in hundreds of parallel conferences, panel discussions, and radio and TV programs organized by parties, unions, churches, schools, and universities. When the final commission report was due, the Green Party authorized a dissenting minority opinion (Sondervotum) that was much more critical of the technology than was the main report. This minority opinion again garnered great attention in the public and the media, and in the interest of balanced reporting it was often given as much space as the main report's conclusions. Thus, anti-biotech activists won the contest of framing. But framings affected all German firms alike, which means that the other part of the puzzle remains:

Where does observed variation in outcomes among firms come from?

There is a striking contrast is between the efforts of BM and BI on the one side, and Hoechst on the other. In 1986 BM and BI were able to build biotechnological production complexes in Biberach and Penzberg, small towns in conservative rural areas in southern Germany. According to media sources, neither facility was strongly contested or even minimally delayed by local opposition. In fact, neither event received much national coverage at all. Hoechst's plan for a facility to produce recombinant insulin near Frankfurt faced fierce resistance from a well-coordinated coalition of Green activists, workers, church groups, and other leftist groups. Hoechst's insulin production became the main showcase event for the opposition to biotechnology and included disruptions at its AGMs, expert reports from the Ökoinstitut, 350 filed oppositions to the plans, and a series of protracted lawsuits that were instrumental in ushering in national legislation in 1990. One highlight was a multiweek "national action campaign against Hoechst," orchestrated by the Green Party in 1986. Hoechst filed for the first permit in 1984, and the facility started operations in 1993.

■ The Corporate Counteroffensive

Did powerful companies like Bayer, Hoechst, and BASF simply succumb to the pressure of activists and public sentiment? Such a view would appear overly simplistic. As one senior executive put it, "We operate in a regulated industry. We are used to politics and being attacked all the time, you only have to think about animal testing, drug prices and so on. We are normally not affected in our decisions by public sentiments and demands."[10]

Lobbying the Government

The German pharmaceutical industry in the 1980s had political clout with local politicians. While they remained moderately successful, their ability to lobby changed with the changing political landscape. Hoechst's experience with an SPD-Green coalition government suggested that pharmaceutical companies needed to contend with a new player on the landscape—the Green Party.

Lobbying yielded two visible successes for the industry collectively. Initially, the SPD had been largely in favor of severe restrictions on biotechnology; pharmaceutical companies were able to split the party by convincing leading unionists that biotechnology was safe for workers and necessary for job creation. Hermann Rappe, the head of the Chemical Industry Union and an influential SPD MP, was an employee representative on the supervisory board of Bayer and instrumental in splitting the union wing of the SPD from the more environmentally oriented segment of the party on that issue. This move deprived the Green Party of a necessary ally to push its agenda in parliaments. The industry association was also successful in narrowing the scope of the genetic technology law passed in 1990 to issues of safety and contamination, thereby limiting a more expansive vision of activists. However, the pharmaceutical companies lost the battle for public opinion.

Public Relations Campaigns

Public relations executives in the German pharmaceutical industry contested the framing efforts of anti-biotech activists, and sought to present biotechnology as safe and scientific. Pharmaceutical companies portrayed biotechnology as the development of medical science, and depicted opposition to it as superstitious and backward. However, they were unable to arouse *emotions* or to offset the emotions triggered by biotechnology critics. As one public relations veteran confessed,

> I went to a panel at the nearest high school with a
> Green member of the state parliament. There were
> 500 people in attendance and it was packed. I was
> winning the argument, and suddenly [his opponent]
> started to scream and cry. So I said to her, "Don't you
> think we should stop being so emotional and be
> more objective/factual about this?" At that point a 50
> year old lady in the audience stood up and said, "Mr.
> [name], are you only a brain or do you actually have
> a heart in this issue, too?" That's when it became
> very clear to me that . . . the problem for the big cor-
> porations is that they are already anonymous and
> faceless, perfect target for activists, you can't win
> with the rational stuff, have to show a human face.[11]

Anti-biotech activists used new tactics that created surprise and confusion in corporations, such as interruptions at AGMs or hostile questions in AGMs that caused executives to become defensive. German pharmaceutical firms also were unable to depict biotechnology as a hotbed of innovation and entrepreneurship. Genetics departments at universities as well as prestigious institutes like the Max Planck Institute did not join the fray, partly because they wanted to preserve their independence from commercial interests and also because a sizable minority within the scientific community of biologists sympathized with the Green movement. Venture capital was exceedingly scarce until the late 1990s, and as a result, there was a dearth of small biotech companies. Thus biotechnology became strongly associated with large pharmaceutical firms that, at the time, were tainted by scandals such as those involving Thalidomide or dioxin.

■ How the Anti-Biotech Movement Affected Decisions at BASF, Bayer, and Hoechst

The anti-biotechnology movement affected the decision-making of BASF, Bayer, and Hoechst managers. Their boards were dominated by chemical engineers averse to uncertainty and concerned about the lingering effects of earlier scandals, as well as scientists troubled by the public debate about biotechnology.

Amplification of Uncertainty

The activities of anti-biotechnology activists amplified uncertainty for decision-makers. To begin with, activists were able to raise a very diffuse sense of uncertainty about the basic viability and safety of the technology. Moreover, movement activists succeeded in creating regulative uncertainty during the second half of the 1980s and into the early 1990s. Finally, the challenges and delaying tactics of activists created uncertainty for the companies regarding the speed with which they could bring products to market and consequently their returns on investment. One biotech researcher explained the following rule of thumb in the industry.

> It's a very simple calculation. Take the total return on any pharmaceutical product over the life cycle. As a general rule,
> - if you go 50% over budget in development costs, the total return drops 10%
> - if you go 50% over budget in production costs, the total return drops 15%
> - if you delay the launch by 1 year, the total return drops 30%
>
> Speed is key in the market we're in. . . . Speed is very critical in biotechnology, because the knowledge turns over so quickly and because patents can very quickly lock you out of a lucrative area.[12]

A board's evaluation of potential biotechnology investments is of course as much driven by the company's business model as by executives' personal knowledge and identities. Companies with large chemical businesses compared the risks and returns of biotech investments to alternative opportunities in chemicals, while pure pharmaceutical companies such as BI, BM, and Schering evaluated alternatives only within pharmaceuticals. Diversified companies such as BASF, Hoechst, Merck AG, and Bayer were also more likely to use a portfolio management approach and hold each business unit accountable for generating positive returns, and thus were reluctant to cross-subsidize early stage developments. As one executive noted, "The question often was, Why spend money on this biotech thing, where we may make some money in 10 years or not, when we could spend it on a chemical product or a product line extension where we can make money within two or three years?"[13]

Heightened Threats to Identity

Anti-biotechnology movement activists were able to frame biotechnology in such a negative light that forays into biotechnology threatened the identities of the firms and their employees. A former executive at Hoechst put the impact of the threat of legitimation on decision-making as follows: "Hoechst had enough on its plate financially and trouble from environmentalists [about chemicals], and didn't want to get even more tainted with opposition to genetics. . . . In Germany, the initial opposition to recombinant technology delayed the launch of recombinant insulin by several years—lost a lot of money on a high volume product."[14]

The negative portrait of biotechnology led to anxious uncertainty among these young scientists. Another informant at Hoechst stated, "There was at a very early stage indeed some debate and uncertainty among scientists about the potential dangers of recombinant cell cultures. It's an issue because you deal essentially with viral material, known to be hard to contain. It was novel stuff. At Behring, we took this very seriously, but you can deal with it."[15]

Some Bayer scientists who were at Berkeley and later

went back to Wuppertal in Germany were disinterested in pursuing biotechnology. The reason was that their children were being exposed in school to the evils of biotechnology by activists who were schoolteachers. These individual-level threats to legitimate professional identities undermined efforts to transfer know-how from foreign biotech subsidiaries and created mixed support within the companies' own workforce. One Bayer executive summarized it as follows: "We built a laboratory in Berkeley, sent people from Germany, but they would come back and not want to work on biotechnology in Germany. The movement was such that our scientists did not tell their kids what they worked on because their teachers would criticize them."[16]

Self-Reinforcing Feedback of Early Decisions

Early decisions and experiences created self-reinforcing feedback loops in which initial failures or successes strengthened or weakened organizations' commitment to a still commercially risky technology over alternative strategic options. Of the firms that made key decisions when they faced high uncertainty and legitimacy threats between 1984 and 1990, BASF/Knoll appears to have ended up lacking the commitment to carry through a technology-focused strategy in the face of opposition from local activists and commercial setbacks. Knoll had been developing Tumor Necrosis Factor Therapy (TNF) as a potential cancer treatment since 1985. While early trials of this potentially quite lucrative drug looked promising, phase III clinical trials were disappointing and development of the drug was terminated in 1993. A year later, and in the face of several years of only marginal profitability with very high R&D expenditures, BASF fundamentally changed its strategy and focused on its strengths in galenics (pharmaceutical technology) and drug delivery instead. BASF sold its pharmaceutical business in 2000. Similarly, in the late 1980s Bayer had to turn down offers to in-license recombinant EPO and t-PA (tissue plasminogen activator) because they lacked the ability to produce them, a consequence of their decision to avoid approval risks in Germany. However, this in turn deprived the company of a potential revenue stream that could be clearly linked to biotechnology investments. Hoechst made pivotal decisions at the onset of the anti-biotechnology movement but was vulnerable because the movement was politically strong in the state where it was headquartered.

In contrast, BM was a very early entrant and had established facilities and expertise before the movement gained strength. It had the added advantage that because of its location, it faced a weaker movement during the peak period. BI continuously expanded its highly profitable biofermentation facilities in Germany and Austria to produce as licensees of other companies. Both Bayer and Hoechst, which also failed to generate revenues early on because of the opposition of movement activists to its insulin and EPO plans, later entered the more immediately profitable and less risky generics market instead. BI and Schering also had the benefit of being located in a state where the anti-biotechnology movement was weak and the government was hospitable. As a result, BM, BI, and Schering experienced some early successes, while Hoechst and BASF/Knoll had early negative experiences and Bayer's case was mixed.

Lock-in of Initial Location Decisions

The large companies affected by the anti-biotechnology movement also decided to locate their biotechnology operations overseas and thus seemingly evaded opposition in Germany. In 1988, Bayer set up production operations in Berkeley, Hoechst invested in a recombinant insulin facility in France (at Roussel-Uclaf), and BASF/Knoll decided to locate its main future biotechnology research center in the greater Boston area. Yet shifting biotechnology investments abroad during the period of strong movement opposition proved consequential, because initial choices locked organizations into locations as subsequent investments were more often used to expand existing initial locations rather than create new ones in Germany.

As biotechnology activities became located at foreign subsidiaries that were not originally designed to perform the full range of drug development and commercialization, these activities became distant from the centers of power and were vulnerable to intra-organizational barriers. For example, at Bayer, different aspects of biotechnological research, development, production, and marketing became distributed across several business units in the United States instead of being more tightly and routinely coordinated by central R&D in Germany. Bayer's U.S. operations came about when it acquired several acquisitions of manufacturing plants and greenfield sites. It operated conventional biotechnology production facilities and performed some genetics research at its Miles subsidiary in Elkhardt, Indiana, had created capacities to produce recombinant Factor VIII at Cutter Labs in Berkeley, California, and ran its conventional diagnostics business out of Ames in North Carolina. Between 1983 and 1990, Bayer had also created a new R&D center in New Haven, Connecticut, which was funded by the pharmaceutical unit, not least via the U.S. sales of one of Bayer's main blockbuster drugs, Cipro. One manager described the history of a biotechnological discovery made in the New Haven lab at a unit focusing on applications of biotechnology to diagnostics. An antibody discovered there had to be marketed and its further development funded by Ames, as Bayer's North American diagnostics subsidiary. However, Ames had no production capabilities, was only marginally profitable as a unit, and hence was very focused on its bottom line. On the other hand, Bayer's therapeutics division in New Haven had a blockbuster drug in Cipro that generated enough money. Cutter Labs was small and focused on hemophilic therapeutics. Miles had little experience with medical biotechnology of the type required for this product but ended up developing the production process in a complex arrangement with Ames, Miles, and the New Haven unit. It took ten years to get this product to market, quite long for a diagnostic product.

Such a constellation was not uncommon. Since foreign units had traditionally been treated as satellites of the main German divisions, they had little experience working with each other and often did not have skills that spanned the entire value chain ranging from research and development to marketing. Initial coordination costs were therefore high.

Because these subsidiaries were also treated as independent profit centers by headquarters, incentives for coordination and transfer were low. Hoechst faced similar dilemmas. One informant summarized Hoechst's solution to the coordination problems and the continued structural incentives working against that solution as follows:

> The solution at Hoechst was to create decentralized research groups that focused on therapeutic areas, so vaccines and blood at Behringwerke in Marburg, cardiovascular in Frankfurt, antibiotics in France. Each would take overall responsibility for all aspects within their areas. That was complicated by working against a very bottom-line driven headquarters: pharmaceuticals were high margin within Hoechst, and Hoechst struggled to make money, so why reduce the margins of these units by pumping money into a technology with remote returns. The squeeze became harder the fewer good products we had and the thinner the pipeline, there was great pressure to make money, and biotech products are often not very high volume.[17]

■ Implications

Much of the impact of social movements on social change comes via their impact on *organizational* policy and practice. Social movements lead to the formation of new understandings, new theories, and new sentiments, and these understandings and sentiments can penetrate and even become constitutive of organizational life. By the same token, organizations can also seek to counteract and influence understandings and sentiments, with more or less success.

This chapter shows how social movements shape the trajectories of technologies by influencing the choices of organizations. A small group of determined market rebels could gain a decisive advantage by framing biotechnology as dangerous, unsafe, and risky. Core activists were able to arouse fear and anxiety and gain a following among private citizens, scientists, politicians, and schoolteachers, who carried these concerns into German pharmaceutical firms through a multitude of entry points. In states where the movement was strong, it was able to create an adverse legal and regulatory climate for biotechnology.

The anti-biotechnology movement exerted asymmetric effects on German pharmaceutical firms. Firms located in states where the Green Party, a key ally of the anti-biotechnology movement, was powerful were exposed to pressure from the movement—hence Hoechst was particularly vulnerable. By contrast, firms such as BI and BM were located in states such as Bavaria or Baden-Württemberg where the anti-biotechnology movement was weaker and lacked access to the political system. They were consequently more propitious places to pursue biotechnology. Moreover, although the larger German pharmaceutical firms such as Bayer and Hoechst were used to dealing with negative public opinion, they were less effective than before because of the unconventional tactics of movement activists, which included highly effective use of the media and grassroots to influence the population and politicians across the conventional spectrum. By contrast, privately held firms such as BI were under the radar screen of activists. Prominence (as proxied by size and visibility) may be more of a liability than an asset in organizations' struggle for control over their technology decisions.

The movement also interacted with the internal routines and decision-making in large German firms. Large German firms had boards dominated by chemists rather than pharmaceutical executives; the chemical business was predictable and precise in calculating returns on investment, while the pharmaceutical business was unpredictable. When movement activists portrayed biotechnology as an assault on nature and linked it to eugenics, top managers of Hoechst, BASF, and Bayer who were coping with environmental scandals in their chemical units sought to avoid further trouble. German executives who were concerned about lengthened payback periods diverted resources to safer chemical and generics businesses. Even when they established biotech facilities abroad, these firms were unable to transfer knowledge due to intra-organizational barriers, and scientists were reluctant to work on these projects.

If the anti-biotechnology movement in Germany is an example of how market rebels penetrated large firms and prevented them from commercializing their technologies, the organic foods movement in Germany presents a striking example of a movement that has successfully penetrated some large organizations (retail chain stores and supermarkets) and induced large German specialty foods firms to develop new products in response to the movement. By contrast, makers of genetically modified foods have been on the defensive in response to the confluence of the organic foods movement and the movement against genetically modified foods. If the organic foods movement emphasizes local foods, the campaign against genetically modified foods spans multiple countries and targets multinationals selling genetically modified food and genetically modified seeds. Even when diversified multinational firms such as ConAgra, Monsanto, or Bayer face a diversified cross-national movement, there are likely to be asymmetric effects because the strength of the movement varies across nations and interacts with the internal culture of different firms in different ways.

From Exit to Voice: Advice for Activists

In his influential book *Exit, Voice and Loyalty,* Albert Hirschman suggested that individuals had three options when dealing with dissatisfaction: to leave, to express one's preferences, or to remain loyal. For Hirschman, exit was the principal choice in markets because withdrawal from a market by individuals was a more powerful signal than the complaints of individuals to producers.[1] Hirschman's formulation emphasized exit as an individual response to dissatisfaction, and failed to take into account the collective dimension of voice—for economists, after all, markets are simply mechanisms to coordinate individual preferences, which rely on prices as signals. In the late 1960s, when Hirschman was writing, "entirely new channels of communication for groups, such as consumers, which have had notorious difficulties in making their voice heard," such as Ralph Nader's consumer watchdog group, were just emerging, but Hirschman didn't explore them in detail.[2]

The detailed histories of several markets presented in this book show that collective voice shapes markets by activating new identities through hot causes that arouse emotions and create a community of members, and through cool mobilization that allows participants to realize collective identities. We considered a wide range of market rebels— auto enthusiasts, home-brewing aficionados, chefs and culinary journalists, owners of mom-and-pop stores, investor

gadflies and institutional investors, and scientists and Green
Party members. While we usually think of market rebels as
some version of Molotov cocktail–throwing WTO opponents, market rebels may be consumers, executives in producing firms or trade associations, or professionals located
in field-wide organizations.

All of them must figure out whether to concentrate their
efforts on changing beliefs or behaviors—the so-called B2B
problem. Hot causes and cool mobilization overcome the
B2B dilemma; hot causes mobilize passions and engender
new beliefs, and cool mobilization triggers new behaviors
and allows for new beliefs to develop. What are the lessons
that can be learned from our case histories? How do activists
create *hot causes* and *cool mobilization*?

Consider an episode that has all of these crucial ingredients: the Swadeshi (home manufacturers) movement in
India, which in 1905 sought to protect a village-based cloth
industry based on artisanal techniques from mill-made
British cloth. The hot cause was the British viceroy Lord Cur-
zon's partition of the province of Bengal along religious lines
in 1905. Both Hindu and Muslim leaders denounced it as a
divisive effort to pit the peasant Muslims in the villages of
eastern Bengal against the more urban middle-class and
land-owning Hindus of west Bengal who were becoming
radicalized. The attempt at partition aroused feelings of
anger, indignation, and outrage. Cool mobilization hinged
on an insurgent and improvisational act—the boycott of im-
ported British cloth from Manchester. It created the space for
urban Indians to support artisanal weavers making coarse
Indian cloth known as *khadi*.

Cloth was a powerful symbol—it signaled the wearer's status—and it served as a pledge of future protection. Activists urged consumers to boycott British mill-made cloth and burn their British-made clothes. The renunciation of British factory-made cloth and the burning of the factory-made cloth in public ceremonies allowed consumers to affirm their Indian identity and solidarity with artisanal producers. People who had never read newspapers, never listened to the radio, and never gone to school joined the mass burnings and were fired with a new sense of collective identity.[3] What made burning British cloth and wearing coarse Indian cloth cool was that it was a shared experience symbolizing the embrace of the simple and the authentic.

The Swadeshi episode, with its emphasis on burning British cloth, nicely illustrates how collective action overcomes the B2B dilemma. Like other social movements, the Swadeshi movement featured a physical assembly of individuals that increased co-presence, a common focus of attention through shared activities that led to a collective sense of the group identity and feelings of solidarity. This inspires emotional energy and enthusiasm in individuals, engendering shared feelings of morality and inspiring additional action and questions.[4] Thus, both hot causes and cool mobilization are gut things. What makes a cause hot is the emotions it awakens and the beliefs it disturbs, and what makes mobilization cool is that it signals insurgency and a distinctive identity. Market rebels are not cool-hunters selecting the next cool thing; instead, they *produce* cool—out of shared emotions and actions.[5]

■ Hot Causes

Causes that lack heat fly below the radar—they do not arouse intense emotions or mobilize public opinion. A cause needs to be made hot, especially when the grievances or issues underlying the cause spill over across multiple jurisdictions or professions. Consider the alternative dispute resolution movement, which arose in response to mismanaged procedures, the overloading of courts, and a reliance on litigation to solve problems. These grievances cut across multiple audiences—judges, social work agencies, mental health agencies, community organizations, bar associations, and the Justice Department. Unfortunately, the cause of dispute resolution never gained much traction because it was a cool cause. Potentially interesting solutions such community mediation, which sought to reserve only the major disputes for courts and use the community to resolve other disputes, and the multidoor courthouse, which opened up channels such as night prosecutors and urban courts to handle cases, gained the attention of legal professionals and social work professionals but did not excite the imagination of the public.

Saul Alinsky, the famed radical, astutely summarized the link between hot causes and emotions in his counsel to rebels and offered the following rules.

1. *Pick the target, freeze it, personalize it, and polarize it.* The opposition must be singled out as the target and "frozen."
2. *Ridicule is man's most potent weapon.* It is almost im-

possible to counterattack ridicule. It also infuriates the opposition, who then reacts to your advantage.

3. *Never go outside the experience of your people.* When an action is outside the experience of the people, the result is confusion, fear, and retreat.

4. *Wherever possible go outside of the experience of the enemy.* Here you want to cause confusion, fear, and retreat.[6]

The tussle between the microbrewers and industrial brewers illustrates all four of Alinsky's rules. These rules imply that causes become hot when they are popularized through simple, unconventional, salient, and authentic methods and experiences. Microbrewing enthusiasts went outside the experience of their enemy by personalizing them as Big Beer and ridiculing them for tasteless, inauthentic beer. They stuck to the experience of their core constituency—home brewers—by arguing for small-scale and artisanal production of beer. The anti-biotechnology activists also illustrate the four rules. They relied on attention-grabbing tactics to highlight the risks of genetic engineering to their constituency (for instance, coming dressed as misshapen apples to village fairs), went outside the experience of their opponents by resorting to blockades and petitions, personalized their targets as throwbacks to Nazi eugenics, and ridiculed them for being unable to forecast the risks of biotechnology.

A key element in packaging hot causes is exploiting unexpected events and issues that crystallize grievances. Such lightning rod issues, as the sociologist Jim Jasper notes, can be the source of moral shock that arouses deep moral feelings of outrage or shame, which provide an impetus for individuals to act and to join in the collective enterprise. For example, investor rights activists exploited large executive compensation contracts, such as the one negotiated with Robert Nardelli, the former CEO of Home Depot, to organize protests and launch anti-management resolutions in shareholder meetings.

■ Cool Mobilization

Cool techniques of mobilization are oppositional, dramatic, and insurgent—they need audience participation to be filled in and to be learned. By contrast, cold techniques of mobilization typically involve the head of the audience and not the heart of the audience—they seldom engage people in creating a sense of community.

Charles Tilly provides a wonderfully clear account of what makes mobilization cool. He outlines four organizing principles that sustain social movements under the acronym WUNC.[7]

1. Worthiness: A cool technique of mobilization has to improve the sense of collective identity and, by implication, the self-worth of participants.
2. Unity: A cool technique of mobilization also has to foster feelings of solidarity and community. Once again, collective identity is central. It is not only symbols such as badges but shared behaviors that inculcate unity.

3. Numbers: A cool technique of mobilization has to involve large numbers of people to display potency. It also requires mobilizing structures ranging from informal groups to formal organizations to enlist recruits.

4. Commitment: A cool technique of mobilization also has to elicit commitment from participants. When participants undertake new behaviors ranging from proselytizing for a cause to displaying symbols, their commitment to the cause increases.

Tilly's arguments imply that cool mobilization derives its strength from the interaction of worthiness times unity times numbers times commitment.[8] For example, "trade at home" campaigns were powerful ways to sustain WUNC in the anti–chain store movement and to mobilize the local community against the onslaught of chain stores. Similarly, the investor rights movement seized on anti-management resolutions to sustain WUNC among investors.

■ **Implications**

Social movements, as Tilly observes, emerged as a new repertoire in Western Europe after the 1750s and were facilitated by the growth of democracy.[9] For much of the twentieth century, social movements have had a powerful and pervasive impact on markets. In the United States, housewives' leagues were progenitors of the consumer rights movement that spawned *Consumer Reports* and eventually paved the way for Ralph Nader and transformed markets for consumer durables.

The standards movement after World War I led to the creation of common industrial standards, which altered markets for industrial products. More recently, the green movement has begun to affect the design of numerous products and services, and the disability rights movement has had a substantial effect on the design of buildings and appliances. The impact of movements on markets is not just a North American idiosyncrasy or a Western European regularity. As I write this chapter, a new fitness movement is sweeping Asia and reshaping the market for foods and exercise machines, and farmers are battling genetically modified foods in Asia and South America. And somewhere, a group of market rebels are tinkering with their hobby, setting the groundwork for a revolutionary new product.

Social movements are an opportunity for organizations. Sagacious executives can capitalize on preexisting movements. Consider two examples. But for the running movement powered by the track coach Bill Bowerman of Oregon, the doctor Frank Cooper, who pioneered aerobics, athletes like Frank Shorter, and a network of running clubs that dotted the country, there would not have been a Nike. Phil Knight, the founder of Nike, was a runner who trained under Bowerman, and the two of them started a firm called Blue Ribbon Sports in 1962 to sell running shoes to athletes at track meets. In 1972, the firm was renamed Nike and eventually exploited the running movement and, later, the fitness movement. In California, the environmental movement has had a powerful effect on making climate change a hot cause and hybrid cars into a cool solution. Toyota capitalized on that with its Prius—so much so that the Prius has become a signal of identity of an owner who cares about his or her environmental footprint.

Social movements also pose threats for organizations. The anti-tobacco movement drew on a coalition of health researchers and attorneys who played a central role in placing restrictions on the market for cigarettes. Similarly, the organic food movement, which emphasizes an alliance between environmentalists and proponents of locally available foods, has created a formidable challenge for food companies purveying standardized and homogenized products to customers.

The challenge for managers is to stop thinking like bureaucrats and to start thinking like insurgents. French generals chastened by the experience of World War I developed the Maginot Line—a line of large forts interspersed with small forts protected by mine fields and anti-tank ditches to ward off a German attack. The assumption was that the Ardennes were impenetrable and would serve as an extension of the man-made Maginot Line. The German forces shocked the French by using the blitzkrieg—a "lightning war" powered by light tank units supported by infantry and airplanes—and simply drove through the Ardennes and went around the French fortifications. The Maginot Line was not simply a physical infrastructure but a mentality that immobilized French defense forces into complacency. Executives in organizations need to overcome a Maginot Line mentality if they are to nimbly capitalize on the opportunities generated by social movements or to deftly respond to the threats posed by movements.

Notes

1 From the Invisible Hand to Joined Hands

1 Fred Turner, *From Counterculture to Cyberculture* (Chicago: University of Chicago Press, 2006).

2 S. Levy, *Hackers: Heroes of the Computer Revolution* (New York: Viking, 1984), 27.

3 *People's Computer Company*, October 1972.

4 For a discussion of whether radical innovations sustain incumbent firms or disrupt their dominance, see Clayton Christiansen, *The Innovator's Dilemma* (Cambridge, MA: Harvard Business School Press, 1997), and Rebecca Henderson, "Underinvestment and Incompetence as Responses to Radical Innovation: Evidence from the Photolithographic Alignment Equipment Industry," *Rand Journal of Economics* 24:2 (1993): 248–61.

5 For an early and valuable formulation, see Paul DiMaggio, "Interest and Agency in Institutional Theory," in *Institutional Patterns and Organizations: Culture and Environment*, ed. Lynn G. Zucker (Cambridge, MA: Ballinger, 1988).

6 Indeed, sociologists have given such short shrift to how social movements transform markets that an influential review argued that the challenge was to "show more comprehensively the value of applying the constructs and mechanisms developed in social movement theory to economic action." Gerald Davis and Doug McAdam, "Corporations, Classes, and Social Movements after Managerialism," *Research in Organizational Behavior* 22 (2000): 195–238. See also Nella Van Dyke, Sarah A. Soule, and Verta Tay-

lor, "The Targets of Social Movements: Beyond the State" in *Research in Social Movements, Conflicts and Change,* vol. 25, *Authority in Contention,* ed. Daniel J. Myers and Daniel M. Cress, (Greenwich, CT: JAI Press, 2004), 27–51. A prominent and early exception is Zald and Berger, who analyzed movement activity in organizations and, by implication, opened up the consideration of markets. Mayer Zald and Michael Berger, "Social Movements in Organizations: Coup d'Etat, Insurgency and Mass Movements," *American Journal of Sociology* 83:4 (1978): 823–61.

7   For research on the diffusion of innovation, see Everett Rogers, *Diffusion of Innovations* (New York: Free Press, 1995). For simple and complex contagions, see Damon Centola and Michael Macy, "Complex Contagions and the Weakness of Long Ties," *American Journal of Sociology* 113:2 (2007): 702–34.

8   Tim Feddersen and David Gilligan, "Saints and Markets: Activists and the Supply of Credence Goods," *Journal of Economics and Management Strategy* 10:1 (2001): 141–79.

9   David Baron and Daniel Diermeier, "Strategic Activism and Non-Market Strategy" (working paper, Graduate School of Business, Stanford University, 2005).

10   Doug McAdam and W. Richard Scott, "Organizations and Movements," in *Social Movements and Organization Theory,* ed. Gerald Davis, Doug McAdam, W. Richard Scott, and Mayer Zald (New York: Cambridge University Press, 2005), 4–40; H. Rao, C. Morrill, and M. Zald, "Power Plays: How Social Movements and Collective Action Create New Organizational Forms," *Research in Organizational Behavior,* vol. 22 (Greenwich, CT: JAI Press, 2000), 239–82. See also Sheldon Stryker, Robert W. White, and Timothy Owens, *Self, Identity, and Social Movements* (Minneapolis: University of Minnesota Press, 2000).

11   Kurt Lewin, "Group Decision and Social Change," in *Readings in Social Psychology,* ed. Theodore Newcomb and Eugene Haretley (New York: Henry Holt, 1947), 340–44.

12   D. P. Redlawsk, "Hot Cognition or Cool Consideration? Testing

the Effects of Motivated Reasoning on Political Decision Making," *Journal of Politics* 64 (2001): 1021–44; J. P. Morriss, N. K. Squires, C. S. Taber, and M. Lodge, "The Automatic Activation of Political Attitudes: A Psychological Examination of the Hot Cognition Hypothesis," *Political Psychology* 24:4 (2003): 727–45.

13 Arlie Hochschild, *The Managed Heart: The Commercialization of Human Feeling* (Berkeley: University of California Press, 1982).

14 J. T. Jost and M. R. Banaji, "The Role of Stereotyping in System-Justification and the Production of False Consciousness," *British Journal of Social Psychology* 33 (1994): 1–27.

15 D. Keltner, D. Gruenfeld, and C. A. Anderson, "Power, Approach, and Inhibition," *Psychological Review* 110 (2003): 265–84; L. Z. Tiedens, "Anger and Advancement versus Sadness and Subjugation: The Effect of Negative Emotion Expressions on Social Status Conferral," *Journal of Personality and Social Psychology* 80 (2001): 86–94.

16 James Jasper, "The Emotions of Protest: Affective and Reactive Emotions in and around Social Movements," *Sociological Forum* 13:3 (1998): 397–424.

17 E. Hatfield, J. T. Cacioppo, and R. L. Rapson, *Emotional Contagion* (New York: Cambridge University Press, 1994).

18 Marshall McLuhan, *Understanding Media: The Extensions of Man* (London: Routledge and Kegan Paul, 1964).

19 Raymond Williams, *Marxism and Literature* (Oxford: Oxford University Press, 1977).

20 Bradley King and Sarah Soule, "Social Movements as Extra-Institutional Entrepreneurs: The Effect of Protests on Stock Price Returns," *Administrative Science Quarterly* 52 (2007): 413–42.

2 You Can't Get People to Sit on an Explosion!

1 Although the origins of the American automobile industry can be traced to George Selden's two-stroke engine design developed in 1879, or to William Morrison's electric car of 1892, or to Ran-

som Olds's steam vehicle purportedly sold to a Indian firm in Bombay, the first firm to make automobiles was set up by the Duryea brothers in 1895. James J. Flink, *America Adopts the Automobile, 1895–1910* (Cambridge, MA: MIT Press, 1970).

2 Cited in Michael Shnayerson, *The Car That Could: The Inside Story of GM's Revolutionary Electric Vehicle* (New York: Random House, 1996).

3 *Munsey's Magazine,* January 1906.

4 *Independent,* June 3, 1909.

5 Paul DiMaggio, "Interest and Agency in Institutional Theory," in *Institutional Patterns and Organizations: Culture and Environment,* ed. Lynn G. Zucker (Cambridge, MA: Ballinger, 1988); Michael T. Hannan and John Freeman, *Organizational Ecology* (Cambridge, MA: Belknap Press, 1989). See also John Meyer and W. Richard Scott, eds., *Organizational Environments: Ritual and Rationality* (San Francisco: Sage, 1993); Neil Fligstein, *The Architecture of Markets: The Economic Sociology of 21st Century Capitalist Societies* (Princeton: Princeton University Press, 2001).

6 Alexis de Tocqueville, *Democracy in America* (New York: Harper Collins, 1966).

7 Flink, *America Adopts the Automobile.*

8 Cited in R. W. Thomas, *An Analysis of the Patterns of Growth of the Automobile Industry: 1895–1929* (New York: Arno Press, 1977), 17.

9 *Scientific American,* August 17, 1895.

10 Flink, *America Adopts the Automobile.*

11 R. F. Karolevitz, *This Was Pioneer Motoring* (Seattle: Superior Books, 1968), 192.

12 *Motor Age,* 1903, p. 3.

13 Flink, *America Adopts the Automobile.*

14 Ibid., 144.

15 *Horseless Age,* February 17, 1904, pp. 196–97.

16 R. A. Smith, *A Social History of the Bicycle: Its Early Life and Times in America* (New York: Heritage Press, 1972).

17 Robert P. Thomas, *An Analysis of the Patterns of Growth of the Automobile Industry, 1895–1929* (New York: Arno Press, 1977), 21.

18 Quoted in Thomas, *An Analysis of the Patterns of Growth of the Automobile Industry*, 21.

19 "The Future of the Motorcycle," *Chicago Times-Herald*, November 28, 1895.

20 Flink, *America Adopts the Automobile*, 42.

21 I took into account the role of other factors such as the interval between one race and another, the number of prior reliability contests, the total number of producers, the average age of producers, the existence of anti-speed incidents, the overlap of winners from one contest to another, the extent of engine diversity (gas versus steam and electric), and cylinder diversity (one, two, three, four, six, and eight cylinders) among producers.

22 Smith, *Social History of the Bicycle*, 149–50.

23 Stuart Chase and F. J. Schlink, *Your Money's Worth: A Study in the Waste of the Consumer's Dollar* (New York: MacMillan, 1928).

24 *Horseless Age*, July 26, 1905, p. 153 (italics mine).

25 I gathered data on potential founders who had a prototype from Beverly Kimes, *Standard Catalogue of Cars: 1805–1942* (Iola, WI: Krause Publications, 1981). I accounted for the effect of the length of time founders had a prototype, whether they used gasoline technology, whether they had prior competences in an allied industry, and the total number of producers and pre-producers combined, and estimated the log odds of potential founders starting operations. For more details, see Hayagreeva Rao, "The Power of Public Competition: Promoting Cognitive and Sociopolitical Legitimacy through Certification Contests," in *The Entrepreneurship Dynamic*, ed. Kaye Schoonhoven and Elaine Romanelli (Stanford: Stanford University Press, 2001), 262–85.

26 Thomas, *An Analysis of the Patterns of Growth of the Automobile Industry*, 47.

27 Robert K. Merton, "The Matthew Effect," *Science* 159 (1968):

56–63. See also Joel Podolny, "A Status-Based Model of Competition," *American Journal of Sociology* 98 (1993): 829–72.

28 John Carlova, "The Stanleys and Their Steamer," *American Heritage Magazine* 10:2 (1959): 40–46.

29 Tocqueville, *Democracy in America*.

30 Michael T. Hannan, Laszlo Polos, and Glenn Carroll, *Logics of Organizational Theory: Audiences, Codes, and Ecologies* (Princeton: Princeton University Press, 2007).

31 Steven Klepper and Elizabeth Graddy, "The Evolution of New Industries and the Determinants of Market Structure," *Rand Journal of Economics* 21 (Spring 1990): 27–44.

3 Evange-Ale-ists and the Renaissance of Microbrewing

1 "Symposium: Did Man Once Live by Bread Alone," *American Anthropologist* 55:4 (1953): 15–526.

2 Solomon H. Katz and Mary Voigt, "Bread and Beer: The Early Use of Cereals in the Human Diet," *Expeditions* 28:2 (1986): 23–34.

3 Victor Tremblay and Carol Horton Tremblay, *The U.S. Brewing Industry: Data and Economic Analysis* (Cambridge, MA: MIT Press, 2005).

4 Joe Bain, *Barriers to New Competition* (Cambridge, MA: Harvard University Press, 1956). See also Klepper and Graddy, "The Evolution of New Industries and the Determinants of Market Structure."

5 Boyan Jovanovic, "Fitness and Age: A Review of Carroll and Hannan's *Demography of Corporations and Industries*," *Journal of Economic Literature* 39 (2001): 105–19.

6 Glenn R. Carroll, "Concentration and Specialization: Dynamics of Niche Width in Populations of Organizations," *American Journal of Sociology* 90 (1985): 1262–83. See also Carroll, Stanislav Dobrev, and Anand Swaminathan, "Organizational Processes of Resource Partitioning," *Research in Organizational Behavior* 24 (2002): 1–40, for a review and for an argument that resource par-

titioning occurs because of the need to customize, anti–mass production sentiment, and conspicuous status consumption.

7 Verta Taylor and Nancy E. Whittier, "Collective Identity in Social Movement Communities: Lesbian Feminist Mobilization," in *Frontiers in Social Movement Theory,* ed. A. D. Morris and C. M. Mueller (New Haven, CT: Yale University Press, 1992), 104–30; Alberto Melucci, "The Symbolic Challenge of Contemporary Movements," *Social Research* 52 (1985): 789–816.

8 Glenn R. Carroll and Anand Swaminathan, "Why the Microbrewery Movement? Organizational Dynamics of Resource Partitioning in the U.S. Brewing Industry," *American Journal of Sociology* 106 (2000): 715–62.

9 William L. Downard, *The Cincinnati Brewing Industry: A Social and Economic History* (Athens: Ohio University Press, 1968), 30–31.

10 Henry David Thoreau, "The Landlord," in *The Writings of Henry David Thoreau,* vol. 5 (New York: Houghton Mifflin, 1906), 161–62.

11 James B. Wade, Anand Swaminathan, and Michael Scott Saxon, "Normative and Resource Flow Consequences of Local Regulations in the American Brewing Industry, 1845–1918," *Administrative Science Quarterly* 43:4 (1998): 905–35.

12 Quoted in "Translator Gains Glimpse of the Past," *Lawrence Journal World,* November 23, 1991.

13 Carl Miller, *Breweries in Cleveland* (Cleveland: Schnitzelback Press, 1998).

14 Tremblay and Tremblay, *The U.S. Brewing Industry.*

15 Carroll, Dobrev, and Swaminathan, "Organizational Processes of Resource Partitioning."

16 See Doug McAdam, "Social Movements and Culture," in *Ideology and Identity in Contemporary Social Movements,* ed. Joseph R. Gusfield, Hank Johnston, and Enrique Laraña (Philadelphia: Temple University Press, 1994), 36–57; Henrich Greve, Jo-Ellen Pozner, and Hayagreeva Rao, "Vox Populi: Resource Partitioning, Organizational Proliferation, and the Cultural Impact of the In-

surgent Microradio Movement," *American Journal of Sociology* 112 (2006): 802–37.

17 Martin Ruef, "The Emergence of Organizational Forms: A Community Ecology Approach," *American Journal of Sociology* 106 (2000): 658–714.

18 Charles Papazian, interview by Dennis Wheaton, Wheaton Report, October 1988.

19 Charles Papazian, interview by Daniel Bradford, *All about Beer,* 2002, http://www.allaboutbeer.com/features/legends1.html.

20 Daniel M. Cress and David A. Snow, "Mobilization at the Margins: Resources, Benefactors, and the Viability of Homeless Social Movement Organizations," *American Sociological Review* 61 (1996): 1089–1109; Suzanne Staggenborg, "The Meso in Movement Research," in *Social Movements: Identity, Culture, and the State,* ed. David S. Meyer, Belinda Robnett, and Nancy Whittier (New York: Oxford University Press, 2002), 124–39.

21 Papazian interview by Bradford.

22 Michael Jackson, interview by Daniel Bradford, *All about Beer,* 2002, http://www.allaboutbeer.com/features/legends1.html.

23 Lew Bryson, "Cleaning the Augean Stables," 2004, http://www.lewbryson.com.

24 Jackson interview.

25 Carroll and Swaminathan, "Why the Microbrewery Movement."

26 Papazian interview by Bradford (italics mine).

27 Carol Stoudt, interview by Dennis Wheaton, Wheaton Report, October 1988.

28 Fritz Maytag, interview with Dennis Wheaton, Wheaton Report, October 1988.

29 Carroll and Swaminathan, "Why the Microbrewery Movement."

30 Cited in Philip Van Munching, *Beer Blast: The Inside Stories of the Beer Industry's Bizarre Battles for Your Money* (New York: Random House, 1997), 247.

31 Carroll and Swaminathan, "Why the Microbrewery Movement," 728.

32 Jean Michel-Vallete and Shaw Millne, *The Craft Brewing Industry: Tapping into the Taste Revolution* (San Francisco: Hambrecht and Quist, 1996).

33 Robert Sullivan, "Head of Steam," *Stanford Magazine* (September–October 1996), http://www.stanfordalumni.org/news/magazine/1996/sepoct/.

34 Jackson interview.

35 Sullivan, "Head of Steam."

36 Carroll and Swaminathan, "Why the Microbrewery Movement," 728.

37 Greve, Pozner, and Rao, "Vox Populi."

38 Steve S. Lee, "Predicting Cultural Output Diversity in the Radio Industry, 1989–2002," *Poetics* 32 (2004): 325–42.

39 Eric Boehlert, "New Life for Little Radio?: Opposition to Big Media Could Invigorate Low-Power FM Radio," July 23, 2003, available at http://www.Salon.com.

40 Greve, Pozner, and Rao, "Vox Populi."

41 Ibid.

42 Ibid.

43 William J. Baumol and William G. Bowen, *Performing Arts, the Economic Dilemma: A Study of Problems Common to Theater, Opera, Music, and Dance* (New York: Twentieth-Century Fund, 1966).

4 The French Revolution

1 Baumol and Bowen, *Performing Arts.*

2 Howard Becker, "Art as Collective Action," *American Sociological Review* 39:6 (1974): 767–77.

3 Hayagreeva Rao, Philippe Monin, and Rodolphe Durand, "Institutional Change in Tocqueville: Nouvelle Cuisine as an Identity Movement in French Gastronomy," *American Journal of Sociology* 108:4 (2003): 795–843.

4 Priscilla Ferguson, *Accounting for Taste* (Chicago: University of Chicago Press, 2004).

5 Andre L. Simon, *A Concise Encyclopaedia of Gastronomy* (New York: Harcourt, Brace, and Jovanovich, 1952).

6 Claude Fischler, *L'Homnivore* (Paris: Odile Jacob, 1993).

7 Rao, Monin, and Durand, "Institutional Change in Tocqueville."

8 Fischler, *L'Homnivore.*

9 Ibid.

10 Rao, Monin, and Durand, "Institutional Change in Tocqueville."

11 Benedict Beaugé, *Aventures de la cuisine française: Cinquante ans d'histoire du gout* (Paris: Nils Editions, 1999).

12 Fischler, *L'Homnivore.*

13 Olivier Nanteau, *Portraits toqués: Enquête chez les trois-etoiles* (Paris: L'Archipel, 1999).

14 Rao, Monin, and Durand, "Institutional Change in Tocqueville."

15 Ibid.

16 David Strang and John Meyer, "Institutional Conditions for Diffusion," *Theory and Society* 22 (1993): 487–511.

17 David Strang, "Cheap Talk: Managerial Discourse on Quality Circles as an Organizational Innovation" (working paper, Cornell University, Sociology Department, 1997).

18 Rao, Monin, and Durand, "Institutional Change in Tocqueville."

19 Ibid.

20 François Simon, interview with Philippe Monin, 2005, Paris.

21 Hayagreeva Rao, Philippe Monin, and Rodolphe Durand, "Border Crossing: Bricolage and the Erosion of Categorical Boundaries in French Gastronomy," *American Sociological Review* 70:6 (2005): 968–91.

22 Jorn Rossing Jensen, "Dogme Is Dead," *The Guardian,* 2002.

23 Katja Hofmann, "Heir of the Dogme," *Financial Times,* 2002.

24 Hayagreeva Rao and Simona Giorgi, "Code Breaking: How Entrepreneurs Exploit Cultural Logics to Create Institutional Change," *Research in Organizational Behavior* 26 (2006): 269–304.

5 Show Me the Money

1 Julie Creswell, "With Links to Board: Home Depot Chief Saw His Pay Soar," *New York Times,* May 24, 2006.

2 R.A.G. Monks and N. Minnow, *Watching the Watchers: Corporate Governance in the 21st Century* (New York: Blackwell, 1996). See also R. Romano, "Public Pension Fund Activism," *Columbia Law Review* 93 (1993): 795–953.

3 Gerald M. Davis and Tracy Thompson, "A Social Movement Perspective on Corporate Control," *Administrative Science Quarterly* 39 (1994): 141–73. See also Michael Useem, *The New Investor Capitalism* (New York: Basic Books, 1996).

4 J. W. Barnard, Institutional Investors and the New Corporate Governance," *North Carolina Law Review* 69 (1991): 1135–87.

5 Diane Del Gurcio, Laura Wallis, and Tracy Woidtke, "Do Board Members Pay Attention When Shareholders Vote No?" (working paper, University of Oregon, 2005).

6 D. Del Guercio and J. Hawkins, "The Motivation and Impact of Pension Fund Activism," *Journal of Financial Economics* 52 (1999): 293–340.

7 W. T. Carleton, J. M. Nelson, and M. S. Weisbach, "The Influence of Institutions on Corporate Governance through Private Negotiations: Evidence from TIAA-CREF," *Journal of Finance* 53 (1998): 1335–62.

8 Nell Minow and Kit Bingham, "The Role of the Corporate Gadfly" (unpublished paper), available at http://www.lens-library .com/info/gadfl.html (accessed March 29, 2000).

9 Robert Monks, speech given at the Symposium on Corporate Elections, Harvard Law School, 2003.

10 J. M. Karpoff, P. H. Malatesta, and R. A. Walkling, "Corporate Governance and Shareholder Initiatives: Empirical Evidence," *Journal of Financial Economics* 42 (1996): 365–95. See also C. M. Daily, J. L. Johnson, A. E. Ellstrand, and D. R. Dalton, "Institutional Investor Activism: Follow the Leaders?" (presented at the 1996 Academy of Management meeting).

11 Yonca Ertimur, Fabrizio Ferri, and Stephen Stubben, "Board of Directors' Responsiveness to Shareholders: Evidence from Ma-

jority Vote Shareholder Proposals" (working paper, Duke University, 2006).

12 T. E. Hill, "Symbolic Protest and Calculated Silence," *Philosophy and Public Affairs* 9 (1979): 83–102, at 84.

13 J. E. Horton and W. E. Thompson, "Powerlessness and Political Negativism: A Study of Defeated Local Referendums," *American Journal of Sociology* 67 (1962): 485–93.

14 C. Knowlton, "Ready for Your Annual Meeting?" *Fortune* 119:9 (1989): 137–42, at 138.

15 Minow and Bingham, "The Role of the Corporate Gadfly."

16 Yuri Mishina, Tim Pollock, Hayagreeva Rao, Jim Wade, and Joe Porac, "The Use of Anti-Management Resolutions by Corporate Gadflies: Choosing Targets for Delegitimation by Peripheral Actors" (working paper, Michigan State University, 2007).

17 D. McAdam, J. D. McCarthy, and M. N. Zald, "Social Movements," in *Handbook of Sociology,* ed. Neil J. Smelser (Beverly Hills: Sage, 1988), 695–737.

18 Mishina et al., "The Use of Anti-Management Resolutions by Corporate Gadflies."

19 Michael Useem, *Executive Defense* (Cambridge, MA: Harvard University Press, 1993).

20 L. B. Edelman, C. Uggen, and H. S. Erlanger, "The Endogeneity of Legal Regulation: Grievance Procedures as Rational Myth," *American Journal of Sociology* 105 (1999): 406–54.

21 Hayagreeva Rao and K. Sivakumar, "Institutional Sources of Boundary Spanning Structures: The Establishment of Investor Relations Departments in the Fortune 500," *Organization Science* 10 (1999): 27–42.

22 Joseph A. Grundfest, "Just Vote No: A Minimalist Strategy for Dealing with Barbarians inside the Gates," *Stanford Law Review* 45 (1993): 857–937.

23 Diane Del Gurcio, Laura Wallis, and Tracy Woidke, "Do Board Members Pay Attention When Institutional Investors Vote No?" (working paper, University of Oregon, 2006).

24 Ibid.

6 Chain Reaction

1 Quoted in Sofronia Scott Gregory, "They Are up against the Wall," *Time*, May 1, 1993.

2 *Ohio State Alumni Magazine*, January 1930.

3 John P. Nichols, *The Chain Store Tells Its Story* (New York: Institute of Distribution, 1940).

4 Paul Ingram and Hayagreeva Rao, "Store Wars: The Enactment and Repeal of Anti–Chain Store Laws," *American Journal of Sociology* 110 (2004): 446–87.

5 Godfrey M. Lebhar, *Chain Stores in America, 1859–1959* (New York: Chain Store Publishing, 1959); Joseph Palamountain, *The Politics of Distribution* (Cambridge, MA: Harvard University Press, 1955).

6 Lebhar, *Chain Stores in America*.

7 Montaville Flowers, *America Chained* (Pasadena, CA: Montaville Flowers, 1931).

8 *National Association of Retail Druggists Journal*, May 21, 1936, pp. 397, 681.

9 Jonathan J. Bean, *Beyond the Broker State: Federal Policies toward Small Business, 1936–1961* (Chapel Hill: University of North Carolina Press, 1996), 5.

10 John Flynn quoted in Charles F. Phillips, "State Discriminatory Chain Store Taxation," *Harvard Business Review* (Spring 1936): 354.

11 *Fortune*, February 1939, pp. 88–89.

12 *Chain Store Progress* 1:5 (1929): 3.

13 Ingram and Rao, "Store Wars."

14 Ibid.

15 Ibid.

16 E. C. Buehler, *Chain Store Debate Manual* (New York: National Chain Store Association, 1931).

17 *Chain Store Progress* 2:10 (1930): 4.

18 *Chain Store Progress* 1 (September 1929): 1.

19 California Chain Stores Association, *The Fifty Thousand Per Cent*

Chain Store Tax (Los Angeles: California Chain Stores Association, 1936), 47.

20 Ingram and Rao, "Store Wars."

21 California Chain Stores Association, *The Fifty Thousand Per Cent Chain Store Tax.*

22 Elmer Eric Schattschneider, *The Semi-Sovereign People: A Realist's View of Democracy in America* (Orlando, FL: Harcourt Brace Jovanovich, 1960).

23 Lauren B. Edelman and Mark C. Suchman, "The Legal Environments of Organizations," *Annual Review of Sociology* 23 (1997): 479–515.

24 Ingram and Rao, "Store Wars."

25 Lee Greenberg, "From Sheep Farmer to Martyr," *Ottawa Citizen*, July 3, 2000.

7 Drug Wars

1 Karen Adelberger, "A Developmental German State? Explaining Growth in German Biotechnology and Venture Capital" (working paper, Berkeley Round Table on Industrial Economies, 1999), 1–29.

2 "In der Biotechnologie hat der Bundesrepublik viel Aufzuholen," *Frankfurter Allgemeine Zeitung*, March 30, 1984.

3 Lisa Baine, "New Biotech Lab to Give BASF Presence in US," *Scientist*, March 19, 1990.

4 Environics International, *Global Public Perception of Food Biotechnology* (Toronto, 2000).

5 Klaus Weber, L. G. Thomas, and Hayagreeva Rao, "From Streets to Suites: The Impact of the German Anti-Biotech Movement on German Pharmaceutical Firms" (working paper, Kellogg School of Management, 2007).

6 Ibid.

7 David A. Snow and Robert D. Benford, "Master Frames and Cycles of Protest," in *Frontiers of Social Movement Theory*, ed. A. D.

Morris and C. McClurg Mueller (New Haven, CT: Yale University Press, 1992), 133–54.

8 Quoted in Weber, Thomas, and Rao, "From Streets to Suites."

9 Ibid.

10 Ibid.

11 Ibid.

12 Ibid.

13 Ibid.

14 Ibid.

15 Ibid.

16 Ibid.

17 Ibid.

8 From Exit to Voice

1 Albert Hirschman, *Exit, Voice and Loyalty: Responses to Decline in Firms, Organizations, and States* (Cambridge, MA: Harvard University Press, 1970).

2 Ibid., 42.

3 C. A. Bayly, "The Origins of Swadeshi (Home Industry): Cloth and Indian Society, 1700–1930," in *Origins of Nationality in South Asia: Patriotism and Ethical Government in the Making of Modern India* (New Delhi: Oxford University Press, 1998), 197.

4 Randall Collins, "Social Movements and the Focus of Emotional Attention," in *Passionate Politics: Emotions and Social Movements,* ed. Jeff Goodwin, James Jasper, and Francesca Polleta (Chicago: University of Chicago Press, 2002).

5 Malcolm Gladwell, "The Coolhunt," *The New Yorker,* March 17, 1997, pp. 78–88.

6 Saul Alinsky, *Rules for Radicals* (New York: Vintage Books, 1971).

7 Charles Tilly, *Why* (Princeton: Princeton University Press, 2006).

8 Ibid.

9 Ibid.

Index

The letters *f* and *t* refer to a figure or table on the page indicated.